I Remember

Indianapolis Youth Write About Their Lives
2013

InWords

I Remember:
Indianapolis Youth Write About Their Lives

Edited by Mark Latta, Darolyn "Lyn" Jones, Barbara Shoup, Corrie Herron, Olivia Gehrich, Brett Hiatt, and James Sandberg

Cover art by Will Watson

Published by InWords: Indianapolis, IN

ISBN: 978-0-9849501-2-6

I Remember

Indianapolis Youth Write About Their Lives
2013

Edited by

Mark Latta, Darolyn "Lyn" Jones, Barbara Shoup, Corrie Herron, Olivia Gehrich, Brett Hiatt, and James Sandberg

InWords

PO Box 30407

Indianapolis, IN 46230-0407

ARTS COUNCIL OF INDIANAPOLIS
SUPPORTED BY THE ARTS COUNCIL AND THE CITY OF INDIANAPOLIS

IAC Indiana Arts Commission
Connecting People to the Arts
This activity is made possible, in part, with support from the Indiana Arts Commission and the National Endowment for the Arts, a federal agency.

Summer Youth Program Fund

LILLY ENDOWMENT + I N C +

The INDIANAPOLIS FOUNDATION
A CICF Affiliate
Inspiring philanthropy

hff

Contents

Introduction

Funded by the Summer Youth Program Fund (SYPF), the Indiana Writers Center's "Building a Rainbow" creative writing program serves a diverse group of young people in Indianapolis, improving their writing and literacy skills through a series of creative writing exercises that teach them how to write the stories of their own lives. The program is named after a colorful, whimsical poster of a half-made rainbow that is covered with tiny stick figures painting, hammering and operating cranes as they work to finish it. The image is a visual reminder that there are many small steps in creating something beautiful - a piece of writing, a dream, a goal, a life.

Working one-on-one, Writers Center instructors, student teachers, and volunteers help the young writers get their words on the page and also encourage them to reflect upon the experiences they've written about, considering how what they've learned can help them make their dreams come true.

I love this program! I love seeing children, heads bent, concentrating hard, writing as fast as they can to make the pictures in their heads into words. I love talking to a child who's stuck, asking questions, making suggestions, maybe even writing a few sentences for her until something in her face changes and she reaches for the pencil to continue her story herself. I love those moments when the program is working just as it should and a certain kind of quiet falls over the room because the children are all lost in the worlds inside their heads. I love how they so often surface, proud and often surprised by what they've written.

I really, really love the show of wildly waving hands near the end of every session, everyone wanting to be first to sit in the Author's Chair at the front of the room to read their stories. And watching them leaf through the published anthologies they receive at the programs' final celebration—real books with their own writing and that of their friends inside.

The world is a difficult, unfriendly place for a lot of these kids. Life is hard. But learning about the power and pleasure of words, learning that with hard work, concentration, and the help of people who care deeply for them and want them to succeed, they can use those words to say something about the world and their lives in it that others want and need to hear.

In this book you will hear their voices. Listen! Enjoy!

And take heart in the honesty, intelligence, compassion, hope and love that shine through these stories. The promise in them makes me believe that these young people will grow up and help make the world a better place.

Barbara Shoup
Executive Director
Indiana Writers Center

Writing Sites

Saint Florian Youth Development Camp

Founded by Indianapolis Firefighters in 1992, the Saint Florian Center provides Indianapolis youth an opportunity to develop leadership skills, problem solving methods, and survival tactics, as well as fostering core values such as honesty, respect, responsibility and character. After-school programs, tobacco-free programs, rites of passage programs, alcohol and violence prevention programs, college preparation programs, and youth ambassador programs are among the services the Saint Florian Center provides for young people.

The Saint Florian Center Youth Development Camp, which serves approximately 100 students each summer, age 6-18, has been in operation for twenty years. Over the course of seven weeks, students learn about the world around them and how to be successful in it by participating in a wide range of activities that include academics, science and technology, team-building, physical fitness and art. This year, Core and Junior Cadets improved their writing skills by writing the stories of their own lives. In 2011, Time Magazine featured the Saint Florian Center Youth Development Camp as an extraordinary summer learning program.

***

La Plaza Leadership Institute for Latino Youth

La Plaza is a groundbreaking effort to be the trusted liaison between Latinos and the larger community. La Plaza exists to serve, empower, and integrate the Latino community of Central Indiana.

The Leadership Institute for Latino Youth (LILY) is a six-week summer leadership program designed to help middle and high school students gain the skills necessary to be better prepared for college, careers and life. LILY accomplishes this goal through math and English enrichment, leadership projects, career and college exploration, physical and health education, field trips, community service and the use of technology.

***

Concord Neighborhood Center

For more than 120 years, Concord Neighborhood Center has been a cornerstone of the south side Indianapolis community. Through social services and educational, recreational and cultural enrichment opportunities, it touches the lives of approximately 4,000 people each year. The Summer Day Camp offers students ages 5-13 an array of activities that involve education, health & fitness, art, music, and the enhancement of social skills. Its overall goal is to provide an engaging environment that accelerates achievement during the months when learning losses most frequently occur.

I Remember
Collected Writing

Trinity P.

Age 7, Saint Florian

Stepdad

I was raised by a generous, cool, nice, sweet, fun stepdad.
I was raised by a dog-loving, kid-loving stepdad.
I was raised by a short, strong, big pointy-haired, yes-no kind of stepdad.
I was raised by a stepdad who loves me and my whole family, especially my mom, even though sometimes they fight. But then they eat and sleep and feel better.
I was raised by a stepdad who will always love me, no matter what, even if I'm bad. Even though the first time I saw him, when I was three, I smacked him in the face.

***

Grapes

Grapes are sweet
They taste like a treat
I eat them all the time.
Sometimes I peel off the purple part
And then eat the sweet middle.
My mom buys grapes
And sometimes I get grapes at my camp.
When I was three years old, I first had grapes;
They tasted sweet
And I loved it
And that's when I first loved grapes.

Imari Q.

Age 7, Saint Florian

New Boots

I got some new boots, they are for winter time.

They're brown with little colored buttons, pink, red, orange, blue, green. They're really comfortable. I don't run in them. They are for winter time.

I only tried on one shoe yesterday. My mom bought them for me. She said, "I bought you some new shoes." I raced over there and said, "I wanna try 'em on, I wanna try 'em on!" I tried them on. Yesterday was a fun day.

They have lots of buttons. I got to try them on. I got to walk around the table and my mom said, "you can only wear them in the winter." She wanted me to try one on and it feels really soft. The inside feels like what's in a pillow. When I put them on, they feel like a prize and I won it. They feel like I was in another state like Florida. Florida is in my boots. When I take them off, it's like they're shouting, "Hooray! Hooray! I got new shoes!"

"I don't want to take off my new shoes."

"Well, you have to. You can only have them during winter."

I felt kind of sad and angry just a little bit.

They felt really good. I mean really good.

***

Oranges

I love oranges. I love how they taste juicy and sour.

My mom helps me peel them. She throws the peels in the trash.

They are orange inside and outside.

The oranges make me think of little balls to throw. The balls don't

Like to be peeled, but the oranges do.

I was 5 and in the house and I went into the car and ate the rest of it.

They make me feel sweet and sour.

Sweet like a rabbit, and sour as a fish!

Salvador R.

Age 16, La Plaza

A Hero

Many people have someone they look up to, or someone whom they admire. Usually this person is referred to as a hero. I look up to a lot of people. Some of those people are teachers, and some are my family members. But there is one person that I look up to. For me he is what I think a role model should be. His name is David Beckham. Ever since I started to watch soccer, I've always wanted to play like him. The way he places the ball on the ground. Then takes three solid steps back. The rest is what makes him a legend of soccer.

***

Salvador
It means lazy, athletic, and nice
It is the number 12
It is darkness and light
It is a soccer ball past the goalkeeper and into the net
It is the memory of David Beckham
Who taught me love and passion
When he played for his team and played soccer
My name is Salvador
It means Practice Makes Perfect

***

The Last Minute Poem

The reason why I named it this is, was because it was literally at the last minute. I really didn't have an idea on what I was gonna do. The teacher just said 10 min left. I started cutting out words. At last I had come up with "The Future is Black n Magical." It was just at random so I really don't know what it means. I found out that a majority of the poems were made at the last minute. If I knew what it means, it will probably mean the future is good but dark at the same time.

3

Desmond R.

Age 12, Saint Florian

I was Raised by a Woman

I was raised by a feisty woman
who taught me how to fight in a Ghetto neighborhood.
I was raised by a woman
who taught me how to defend myself and respect others at all times.
She listens when I need somebody to listen.
I was raised by an African American
that was always in trouble but always provided anyway.
I was raised by a woman who loves purple.
I was raised by a woman who does driving for a living.
I was raised by a woman who can throw down.

***

My First Cruise

I remember my first cruise.
I remember the water.
I remember the friend I made.
I remember swimming every day.
I remember being in a long line.
I remember the 20 pieces of ice cream I had.
I remember being there with family.

Michelle S-R.

Age 12, La Plaza

Music

I love loud music. It's like the loud music refuels me from a hard day of work. It carries me away to a whole new universe where you can kiss all of your worries away; a place where you can let go, and be yourself and not try to be perfect and impress lots of people; a paradise where you can release your thoughts, and be you and stop trying to be Ms. Perfect and impress her kingdom.
Instead focus on you. Who is the true you? Show your true colors.

***

Dead

Two of the many things I could not live without are my phone and my charger. They are the things that keep me connected to the world of communication and conversations. Since I am shy in class I text people instead what I feel and think. I just ask for your number and it's set. I need the charger to regenerate my phone's energy and awesomeness.

I think that it means to me that I don't get to get out much so I text and call instead because my mom works a lot and so does my dad so I have to stay and babysit my little sis so that's why I text and call. And my phone means a lot to me. Also because if I am in trouble, I call and call for help if I get jumped.

I am a charger 'cause I like to recharge people from sad to happy battery. I am a charger 'cause I like to recharge people's batteries from low to super high. I give life. I reconnect you to the world once again every day.
But electricity is the start to life.

James Sandberg

Student Teacher, Saint Florian & La Plaza

Each of us has a story to share. This may be cliché, yet the power behind it remains tried and true. Tried in the classrooms whereupon many kids have written the words on these pages; true, as you can see in those words before you.

I believe that part of being human includes a fierce, insatiable desire to be both known and loved. But the fear of self-exposure to the eyes of untrusted others preempts many of our efforts to share our stories with each other. Thus, writing memoir takes on a near-salvific role for many individuals who, while unwilling to share their story with another person, may feel liberated by processing and reflecting upon their personal writings before sharing them with others. Unfortunately, writing like this is hard. It is hard because some of us have brutal stories that are painful to remember, because some of us haven't yet learned to articulate in words the struggles we experience, because some of us simply are not confident enough writers to even attempt writing something so personally significant as our own story. We all need some encouragement. We all need to be told that what we have to say is important, because it is. The stories are powerful, because the authors are powerful.

The authors of this anthology all wield the powers of expression, of originality, of honesty, of imagination and of self-assuredness; powers that often diminish with youth. We adults have so much to learn from them. Whether the content of the writing is a favorite meal or one's own name, a pair of shoes or a lost family member, these authors have each shared part of themselves with the readers of this book, with you, with the world.

To be listened to, appreciated, valued, respected, learned from: this is what the writers need, and this is what they demand of us by offering their work.

Let's read closely, let's see their world through their eyes, let's join in their narratives and become part of a bigger story of a greater community of sharers and story-tellers. We owe this to them. We owe this to ourselves.

Listen.

Nia D.
Age 8, Saint Florian

I Remember...

I remember when I went to the firehouse with my Girl Scout troop, and we got in the fire truck and went down the pole and saw the ambulances.

I remember when I went to Chicago. We got on a taxi boat. It was yellow, and it took us to Chinatown. It was fun. We got pizza. It was cheese. Then we went back to the hotel.

I remember when I went to my cousin's funeral. He got shot, and he was sixteen. He was from Elkhart. I still miss him a lot.

***

Sacred Places

My sacred place is North Carolina. There are lots of trees and mosquitos. It was very hot outside, so me and my cousins had a water gun fight. I won. My cousin's name was Addison and her brother's name was Eyligah. My cousin's mom was soaked. She was mad so she got a water gun and sprayed us. We had fun the next day. We went to the college, and they had a store. At the store, me and my brother got a hat and a bear. My dad got two hats. My mom didn't get anything because she already had a hat at home. I liked it because I had fun, and I got to see my family.

.

Isaiah D.

Age 8, Saint Florian

Shoes

I remember when I bought my favorite shoes from the shoe store. They are very colorful. The colors in my shoes are blue, black, yellow, green, gray, gold, purple, pink, and red. They have a nice design on the bottom and they make me jump on and off tables. They are squishy and crushy as well with yellow shoe strings. I have had these shoes for 8 weeks and they are getting way too small. They are tight on my feet now because I am getting bigger but they will always be my favorite shoes. Forever. THE END!

***

One time there was an old man with small shoes and a cat. THE END.

***

Plane to Mexico

I remember that I went to the airport with my mom. I rode the plane first. I went up in the air in July. It was fun. It made me feel sick. It feels scary and I was sitting with my brother James. I drank an apple juice and I flew again on an airplane. I knocked on the pilot's door and nobody answered. They said, "everybody in your seats." I was really sad cause I couldn't talk to him, the pilot. I flew to Mexico! It was bigger than the whole school. The plane was green. The plane wasn't green, the wings were green. It was bigger than the football stadium.

Davia T.

Age 9, Saint Florian

Sacred Place

My sacred place is the beautiful, peaceful, amazing beach. The sand going between my toes, the wind whipping my hair, the waves pushing me back. It was in Florida and the beach's name was the Coco Beach. Me and my family go there every year. It was so relaxing and peaceful. Me and my family collected shells. We collected thirty-four shells in total; that is a lot of shells and I have all of 'em. That was when my family and I went on our vacation. We was on our school break. So when we went to the beach with my brothers, sister, and my mom and dad and me and we brought my brother David and my sister Sydney Banks. It smells like fresh air and water. It smells like the ocean. We stayed for six days in Florida. It was hot and every time I got hot, I went back in the ocean to cool down. And every time I got sand on me I went to get back and the pool again. I love when I went to the beach-- it was the best vacation ever. We took pictures.

***

Like Syrup on My Pancakes

I was raised by my great parents who are sweet like honey. They say to me every single day before I go to bed, and before I go to camp, "I love you no matter what." I was raised by magnificent parents. My dad looks like a prince and my mom looks like a queen. They also treat me like a princess. I feel so spoiled. My mom and dad are like the syrup on my pancakes. They call me Sweetie because they say I am sweet to them. Sometimes they call me freckles cause they love my freckles. I love my parents like they are heaven. I will never let them go even when they die or they get sick they are never going to leave my heart.

Dayron T. Jr.

Age 12, Saint Florian

With My Name Tattooed

I was raised by a woman with red hair. A woman with my name tattooed on her arm with a Bugs Bunny character. I was raised by a woman that loved to spend time with her kids, by a woman who loved to eat pizza. I am raised by a woman who wanted to move back to Indianapolis. I am raised by a woman who can sing.

***

My LeBrons

My LeBrons are black and red. My shoe strings are black and they have his signature on the bottom. They have his logo: a lion with red eyes. I got them for winning my first basketball game. My Dad got them for me at Footlocker. The name of our team was the Celtics. We had names like the NBA. We were under pressure and I had to go to the free throw line and I made the first free throw but missed the second one that put us in debt, and they missed a 16-footer, and I got rebound, and I called a timeout with ten seconds left on the clock. Then I got the ball behind the 3 point line; my teammate said, "Shoot the ball!" The crowd yelled, "5-4-3-2-1!" I shot at 3; it rolled around the rim, then it went in and I yelled, "Let's go!" really loud.

Cortez T.

Age 12, Saint Florian

My Baby Brother, Jayce

I walk off the bus toward my house my heart filled with anger because things weren't going so well at school, so then I feel like I want to just be alone. Then I walk through the door and hear only dead silence; then I see a glistening wonder in my mother's hands. Then she gives the baby to me, and I feel his soft cheeks and his smooth hands. Then I smell a scent and it smells like roses. Then I smell my brother and I know it's him. Then the sight of him makes me start to cry; then I say to myself these are tears of joy, my brother looked like a beautiful baby wrapped in a blanket. Then my heart is filled with happiness. I knew my mom was having a baby, but I didn't know she was coming home today. I was so so excited and that anger was way long gone.

***

The Voice of an Angel

I was raised by a hairstyling fashion coordinated Christian from Indianapolis who loved her kids like the way she had a craving for string beans. My mom is a hugger who gives bear hugs and hates Ramen noodles like nasty peanut butter. My mom raised me to be a loving careful and leading godly man. My mom is the kind of woman who wants to go off on you over something little and she is the woman who gave me my pacifier when I was crying. My mom showed me one way to defend myself in a problem. She tells you straight, "No play game." She is a confident and loving mother. My mom has the voice of an angel. I love you mom; you raised me.

11

Darrick T.
Age 10, Saint Florian

Stepdad

I was raised by a stepdad who stepped up to the plate when my dad couldn't, and I appreciate him for that because my father has a really bad temper and he gets mad over silly things, such as a video game called Call of Duty: Black Ops 2. When I play the game, he wants me to do everything. He wants me to do everything. He wants me to play the games he does, but I don't want to, but he camps in corners, and I rush so he says he wants me to be a camper, but I don't.

***

I Remember

I remember when I had a horse.
I remember when I had a pet goat named Billy Bob.
I remember when Desmond threw a ball of paper at Kelly. LOL
I remember when I lost Bob the Builder was gone.

I remember when I had a pet named Billy Bob and he was a very loyal and we'll always be together so we had to move and Billy Bob had to gooooooo.

Taiche R.

Age 13, Saint Florian

Outside My House

I remember when my mom and I pulled up in the car in front of my house and
They, the Africans, were yelling.
I remember when they were throwing beer bottles everywhere.
I remember when they walked over by our car;
I was mad that they were in front of my house breaking glass.
I remember when this girl started hitting the other girl.
Cusswords, people yelling, gibberish,
A nasty most unclean booty smell.
I saw glass. I was trying to get in my house.
I was laughing because one of the brothers was jumping around yelling, "Oh!
Oh!" He was holding the girl back and trying to hit the girl.
And my mom said you can't hit a girl.
Lots of people were watching.
The police pulled up and everybody ran.
One girl fell and the police started running after them.
They started running towards the park.
My mom told me not to grow up and be like that because
Your actions are the cause of your future.

Anthony R.

Age 13, La Plaza

My Teacher, Mrs. Rush

Mrs. Rush. I liked that teacher because she was caring, helpful and sometimes funny. I was in Grade 3 and no, she was not strict, she was nice. She taught me the times table and division table. She always told me to do my best and when I had errors she helped me how to do it.
Her lessons were great.
I learned all kinds of stuff.

***

My Name Is...

My Name is Original for me because it is popular everywhere.
Everywhere I go I hear the name Anthony. I keep thinking it's me but it's not me. I think the name Anthony is an American name and it sounds smoother. Anthony in Spanish sounds kind of forceful because of the "An" sound. In Italy they say "Anthonio." I think the name Anthony is a multicultural name.

***

Deep Down...

Deep down I really want to say that the belly flop really hurt my back and it was red and that's why I went to play basketball.

Eiondra T.

Age 9, Saint Florian

First Shoes

I remember The First Shoes I wore on the First Friday of Fourth grade. They were blue, pink, and orange cowboy boots. I loved those boots but they got too small so I couldn't wear them anymore. I was sad so we gave them to the Goodwill store. I am happy for the girl wearing them. When I first wore them nobody liked them. When I first got them I was 6 years old and I wore a size 3.

***

Sacred Place

A sacred place for me is under my big Tinkerbelle blanket in my room and in the basement. It's not really a blanket, it's a blanket with sleeves. It is a Snuggie; a sweater type blanket. But the back is the front. The places I wear it is everywhere in the house. When I wear it, I dance around the house. I dance to hip-hop music and Justin Bieber.

Marquia T.

Age 11, Saint Florian

I Remember

I remember when
Eye doctor blew air in my eye
My tongue started bleeding
Saying we have $59 in our treasury
I first got a weave, I started 5th grade
I had my first 100 dollar bill
I almost got hit by a car
SFC went to the mall, designing my nails
Starting Core, ending JC
Falling back in my chair, falling off a trampoline
Watching ridiculousness
Getting a hash brown from McDonald's
Eating strawberries with sugar.

***

Michael Jackson Birthday Party

I was raised by the neighborhood my parents and great uncles and aunts grew up in. My grandmother raised my mom and her siblings. My grandmother is my mom's grandma. Everything my mom knows she either got it from Grandmother or Uncle Jason which is her brother. I remember being over at Grandmother's house at the age of four and I was looking at the sky. I told my mom and Grandmother that the sky had a scratch and needed a Band-Aid. To come to notice an airplane and flew by and left dust of air in its position. When I was 7 years old I went to what I thought was the best school ever. (Until I saw it on the news a month or two ago). But sadly I moved and that's when my life on Ruckle started to get a little meh. When it was getting close to my bday which is in March, Grandmother was suffering from cancer. Okay, so it's my party everybody is dressed up in their M.J. gimmicks. Did I mention... I had a Michael Jackson themed 8 bday party! Okay so without noticing Grandmother is dying in the middle of the night. So on March 14, 2010, was the death of Grandmother, but I'll never forget how she raised me.

Ashanti E.

Age 11, Saint Florian

Trip to Holiday World

I remember when I went to Holiday World for the first time. I went with my mom, my auntie Camia, and my three little cousins, Jermaine, Lil Stevia and Kamiya. The first ride we rode was the Raven. It was me, my mom and my auntie. I was scared. My mom was laughing at me and my auntie because we were scared. After, we saw this dude jumping from a high board into some water. Next we went to the water park side of Holiday World so when we got there we went into the pool, and then my mom and auntie went to get something to eat. My auntie's friend watched us. So, when they got back, we ate, and then we went and rode the Mammoth. That was a long line. We were in the line for about 30 minutes. Then we finally got up there to the top, and then right when we got up there, my auntie's friend had told her that her nephew had gotten kicked out of the water park, so my auntie was about to leave, but my mom told her to stay because she waited in this line for nothing. So when we got up there, we got in the boat and it was three of us so we had to have another person because all of us are skinny, so this other lady wasn't skinny so she rode with us. So after we got off we rode other rides and then we left around 9:00. We went to the gas station and got food and then left and went home. We got there around 11:30ish.

The End

Lyrik E.

Age 12, Saint Florian

Food

As I walked into McDonald's with my friends, I smelled the fresh scent of chocolate chip cookies. As I looked around, I worried about if I was going to get some fresh cookies, because sometimes they stay in the little box too long. As I went to stand in the long line, somebody had just ordered the last batch of chocolate chip cookies. As I heard somebody order the last batch of cookies, I got so happy that I hugged my friend so tight that she couldn't breathe. At that time it was our turn to order so I said, "Can I get three fresh chocolate chip cookies with some cold and delicious milk?" When I was done ordering, I sat down. As I was sitting down with my friends, the cashier said, "Three chocolate cookies with milk." I ran so fast to get it that I ran into someone. I hurried up and said, "I'm sorry." I got the bag and sat down. As I opened the bag, I smelled the fresh scent of cookies. I took it out and bit into it. My mind had gone into heaven.

***

I am being raised by...

My mom and dad, who taught me things. They taught me how to respect people and how to be happy. Like a loving and caring mommy and daddy, they teach me how to have a clean house and not dirty. My mommy is one person who I look up to. She teaches me how to go on in life and have a good education. We get our hair done together on Saturday mornings. I love my mommy. My daddy is another person I look up to. He is a funny person. He makes me laugh every time I talk to him. Even when I talk on the phone with him. Even though we don't live together, he teaches me how to defend and control myself. Even when I'm in front of my friends, I will always kiss them.

Anton T.

Age 8, Saint Florian

I Remember

I remember
bike
granny's macaroni
I like cheese
green beans

***

Mommy

Mommy raised me.
Mommy looks like me,
but tall with a
little stomach. Her
hair is brown and
it's long.
Mommy says, "I love you."
When I'm in trouble, she says,
"Get in your room."
Mommy makes me
ham sandwiches
with cheese.
She cooks me food
every day.

Anthony T.

Age 14, La Plaza

The Boring Poem

Well, this is going to be boring.
Boring because I don't know how to write
poems, boring because all I'm going to
be talking about is me not knowing how
to write a poem.
But maybe if I knew how to write
poems I wouldn't be so bummed about
writing one. It's writing class so I guess
that is the main/only reason I'm writing
a poem
One day I'll write a poem;
not because I have to, but because I
wanted to.

***

Anthony C. T.

It means cool, spicy, and curly
It's the number 789,465,995,129,848
It is as cool as the ocean
It is a smile as bright as the sun
It is the memory of Lenabel T.
Who taught me the difference between lies and truth
When she cried because I lied about eating
Taco Bell without her
My name is Anthony C. T.
It means YOLO

20

Lenabel T.
Age 12, La Plaza

Things I Never Want to Do

Die
Get a sun burn
Don't get bullied
Don't want to be a boy
Don't want to get shot
Don't want to work at McDonald's
Don't want to be poor
Don't want to have a poor education
Don't want to lose my family
Don't want to go to jail
Don't want to get kidnapped

***

My Name

My name is special. Since my mother didn't know what to name me she came up with the idea to combine my grandmothers' names so my dad's mom's name is Magdelena and my mom's, mom's is Isabel. So she combined them and made Lenabel J. T. But sometimes my name is so annoying. When I go to school I have to pray they don't say my name wrong. I hate it. My name is either misspelled "Lenabell," said wrong, "Lindabel," and don't get me started with my last name. I hate my last name even though it's my dad's. I get called the following: Turikyios, Turtle, Turqoise, Tortilla. I mean it doesn't even sound like that.

Natalia V-C.

Age 13, La Plaza

Something is like a black and white in the bottom.

***

I am a broken phone. I have frustrated moments and in the frustrated moment I broke my phone.

***

They Showed Me Love

Deep down, I really want to say that I wish I had an older brother because I could tell him everything. For example, if I was sad, I like could tell him why I'm sad and he could take me to so many places. I would tell him everything. So he could give me advice about everything. He would have been my best friend that would understand me. He could defend me, care about me, and etc. I just wish a lot I would have had a brother.

My Grandparents raised me when I was little. My parents were in U.S while I was in Mexico. My Grandparents raised me up. For me *raised* and *took care of me* is the same because raised shows you respect and took care is just like they took care and are showing respect. I'm thankful that my Grandparents raised me. They showed me love. I love my Grandparents and once again I'm thankful about raising me up, while my parents work hard in the U.S.

I never want to end it because I got very close with them. So they are special to me. Also because my friends, they never leave me alone they always make me feel better. I also got a lot of trust on them. So when I don't feel good, I trust them and make me feel better. I also don't want to end it because I love texting, talking on the phone etc. with them. We have great convos. They make me laugh a lot. I just love talking/hanging out with them. They are great friends!

Amaya F.

Age 11, Saint Florian

Sushi
Look L) Sushi
Tastes T) yummy in my tummy
Smells S) fish and soy sauce
Feels F) sticky and cold
Sound S) my mom is with me and we are laughing and talking
Where W) at Trader's Point by Cold Stone

***

Super Dad

It happened this year in 2013 during the summer. I left my lunch and water bottle at home. My camp, St. Florian Center, was going on a field trip to Cincinnati, Ohio to the National Underground Railroad Museum. I was so happy to go, but I guess I was a little too happy because I left my lunch and water bottle at home. I started FREAKING Out. I thought I lost my lunch... (music) dun-dun-duuuuun. Then we were on the bus. As the doors closed, I saw a big arm and hand. It was my dad! He went back home and got my things. I was so happy because my super dad saved the day!

***

A Community Who Loves

I was raised by my mom: beautiful, sweet, funny. My dad: kind, strong, fireman. My sister: loving, caring, sharing. My grandma: fun, peacemaker, awesome food-maker. My grandpa: sleeper, snorer, bold. My uncle: respectful, bald, wise. My aunt: young, tall, poet. My friends: tall, short, hilarious. My teachers: full of knowledge, challenging, strict but loose. So with all that I was raised by a community who loves and cares for me!

Wesley G.

Age 10, Saint Florian

Shoes

My pair of Nikes are green, yellow, black, and red. I've had these shoes for ten months and I have memories with them. I remember when I first got them. I tried them on and they were a size six. I remember when I went to the mall with my shoes. I remember when I had them on at my friend's birthday party. I remember when I went out to eat in these shoes. I remember when I went to the Grand Canyon and I was climbing the mountain and my shoes were hot. They are leather and the leather part is green and the other parts are leather too. These shoes are squishy in the inside and my laces are leather and I also have a Velcro strap on my shoes.

These are high tops and they have a Nike sign on the back and the Nike sign is red and the other one is yellow. I was playing basketball in these shoes. These shoes have been through wrestling and boxing and front flips. I remember when I wore this to Bistown and me and my mom worked there but we had two different jobs. She works at Ray's Recycling and I worked at PNC bank. I went to the Children's Museum.

***

I was Raised by...

I was raised by my mom who is funny, fun, happy, goofy, lovable. My mom would die for me and I would die for her. My mom's dream was to be a hairstylist and a singer. She taught me to respect people and she put a roof on my head and she fed me. My mom loves to make brownies with me. She makes the best.

Tamara V.
Age 12, Saint Florian

I was raised by:
  funny people,
    laugh at loud joke telling has 2 jobs,
    DJs and cooks at a restaurant.

***

Dear Grandpapa

I wish you was here! You left too soon. But, you're up there with the Lord. I am sure you are in good hands. I will be up there with you. You are my best friend, my everything. I love you grandpapa. No matter what happens. We were very close together. We did a lot of stuff together. We played games and singed dance and more. You was important to me a lot. You was right by my side through thick and thin.

At the funeral Shawna, me, and Kamaria sang your favorite song. By Kirk Franklin, *You Don't Have to Worry*. Grandmama was screaming for you. Shawna read a poem for you. Shawna's volleyball teacher preached at your funeral. She preached the funeral grandpapa.

Love,
Tamara
Great-Great granddaughter

Olivia Gehrich

Student Teacher, Concord & La Plaza

Here's to Every 'That Kid'

I remember when my friend moved away in the fourth grade, and I decided to write a short story about what friendship meant to me at the time. My story, The Gift, gained a huge following and renown...within my family. Nonetheless, their support for the trivial musings of an eleven year old ignited the spark I had for a love of writing. My career as an authoress continued into many papers, short stories, drawings, and a newsletter I began as a sixth grader entitled *Rockin' Sixth Grade Extra*. I never knew if my writing embodied any real talent, but my passion far exceeded my doubt. And I believe it is because I was raised by people who believed in my words.

I was raised by cooking and fishing with my grandparents and telling stories about peanut butter-eating dragons while huddled in a big, warm bed. I was raised by proofreading Dad's Youth Group bulletins and writing cards to Mom. I was raised by filming pseudo news segments on a make-believe show with my siblings. I was raised by encouragement and words.

One reason I applied for the position with the Building a Rainbow project is that I believe in the power of words and their ability to build, break, change, and influence the world. Words do not discriminate. They should be viewed as children, nurtured as living things, and when they are adopted to the right families in the right way, magic happens.

"People know what they want to say, but not always how to say it." Whenever I am asked why I tutor writers or work with people on developing papers, this is the answer I give. The reason I stand by this outlook is because it has been proven right time and time again. This is true for writers at all ages and skill levels.

As a tutor on a college campus, my interactions are generally with students in their twenties. Though I felt originally intimidated by the idea of working with writers half that age, I also found myself excited. Finally! Finally I get to work with people before a world of "No" and "You're doing that wrong" crushed all of their creative, imaginative spirits. So often I watch students my own age walk into the Writing Center overwhelmed and apprehensive about the writing process, or worse, students who believe their voice brandishes no meaning. Because somewhere along the line, someone told them they were wrong or their opinion didn't matter. Somewhere along the line, they were told they didn't matter. And somewhere along the line, they believed that was true.

The writers I worked with during the Building a Rainbow project not only restored my faith in humanity, but also restored my faith in myself. I think we've all felt like "that kid." The kid who got it wrong once and never fully recovered. The kid who stopped raising his hand after an incorrect guess earned him a bout of laughter from the class. The kid who closed her journal forever after being told her life wasn't that interesting. This project gave me the opportunity to look into the eyes of some of the world's "that kid's" and realize all they really want is a chance to be heard and have their thoughts validated.

There used to be a show about how kids say the darndest things. After these few weeks, I am here to say that analysis is completely factual. But they don't say the darndest things in that what they say is irrelevant or silly. They say the darndest things in that what they say is extremely powerful, often times in its brevity and raw honesty. Kids see things in a simpler way, which until recently I thought meant it was weaker. This summer, these writers proved me wrong.

Simpler isn't weaker. Simpler is clearer. Simpler is more beautiful. Simpler is stronger. And because of this experience, so am I. So. Thank you, parents. Thank you, sponsors. And most importantly, thank you, writers.

Alannah W.

Age 9, Saint Florian

Is It a Girl?

Once I woke up I saw a baby in my dad's hands. I said, "is it a girl?" My dad said, "No." I was mad because I wanted it to be a girl but I was happy because I didn't have to be the youngest kid.

I said, "What's his name?"

"Kamon," said my mom.

I didn't want to touch Kamon.

Kamon W.
Age 7, Saint Florian

Firefighter for a Day

I remember being a firefighter for a day.
I remember wearing their clothes.
I remember hanging out at the fire station.
I remember when I put out fake fires.
I felt like I was a fireman. I felt happy.
I was all alone.
I was excited.
We got sprayed with the hose.
I was like
ahhhhhhhhhhhhhhhhhhhhhhhhhhhhhhhhhhhhhhhhhhhhhhhhhhhhhhhhhhhhhhhhhmo
mhhhhhhhhhhhhhhhhh.......................

***

Basketball

I remember when I played basketball with my brother over at my cousin's house. It was fun. He could dunk and he blocked all my shots. I said, "That's not fair." I still laughed about it. My favorite thing is to play with my brother. Basketball makes me feel happy.

29

Kayla W.

Age 12, Saint Florian

I Am Raised By

I am raised by
A meditation listening
soul clearing
super green drinking
comfy shoe wearing lady

A banana pudding ice cream loving, sit down and watch movies with me but make sure your room is clean kind of person.

A short, dark haired lady, all black with a pop of color wearing, brown-eyed with a warm smile lady.

A choking on bacon thinking she was gonna die
A laugh with me till our abs hurt, faces are red, tears in our eyes, person.

A lo mein with extra veggies eating, organic food loving, drink water because water is your medicine type of mom.

Meditation listening
soul cleansing
super green drinking
angel hair noodles with
pesto making lady

I am raised by a love you with all my heart no matter what you do when you grow up and you'll always be my baby girl woman.

Angeles Noelle S.

Age 8, Saint Florian

My Shoes

I remember when I got the shoes. I was excited and happy at the same time. They were high tops.

They are gray and purple and they say Air Jordans.

They make me feel happy.

The next day my friends were amazed; they said, "where did you get those shoes?" I said, "Kids Footlocker."

I remember it was a hot day and the ground was very rocky and bumpy.

The sky was sunny and bright, then after a little while it got rainy but we still ate lunch outside. Then we went home.

My shoes still were not messed up.

***

My Special Place

My Special place is my room I sit down on my chair and watch t.v. sometimes. I lie down on my bed and snuggle with my favorite blanket and take a nap. I sit in my chair and do my nails. Sometimes I do my homework in my chair. In the summer I do my work book in my chair. My closet: I pick out all my favorite clothes every day. It also has all my favorite shoes.

***

I Remember

I remember when I went to Universal Studios in Florida. I remember I was wearing a white tank top and blue jean shorts. I remember it was three days ago. I remember it was in Florida. I remember I was with my mom. I remember when we went to the Emeril's restaurant. I remember I had pizza there and the best cookie and chocolate milk and my mom had a big pork chop and it was in 2013.

Me and my mom had the greatest time.

Jordan T.

Age 7, Saint Florian

My Shoes

My shoes look orange and dark gray/gray also
white and they make me feel happy and cool
because they are loose, because my feet can
barely breathe and! yes! they! are! new!!!!!!!!!!

And I also like the style. Before this me and my mom
and I went to target to get my sister some
pants and I wanted to get something too
and we saw the perfect shoes for me so I
tried them on and they fit perfectly and
these shoes that I'm writing about
I'm wearing right now.

***

Mr. Fluffy Pants

This story is about Mr. Fluffy Pants. He's fluffy but small. He has a bushy tail and
it's also big.
Mr. Fluffy Pants feels soft and fluffy.
Mr. Fluffy smells like new, very new.
I play with him at my dad's house and play with it every time I go over there.

Xaveon W.

Age 13, Saint Florian

I Was Raised

I was raised by men and women who are meat eating people. I was raised by men and women that always told me that I had to go to college. I was raised by men and women that helped me with everything.

I was raised by men and women that always said, "never say 'I can't' because you can." I was raised by men and women that are married for 15 years. I was raised by men and women that loved to have fun. I was raised by men and women that always wore shorts and shirt for the men and the women wore pants and a shirt.

I was raised by men and women that loved sports. I was raised by men and women that had 3 kids together and 2 pets, a dog and lizard.
I was raised by men and women that loved their 3 kids, two boys, one girl. I was raised by hard working men and women. I was raised by men and women who I loved.

***

B.B.

I lost my dog a year ago on a Friday night. She died of cancer. My mom found her in the space behind the couch. I was stunned. I knew she had cancer but I didn't know she would die so soon. She was here before I was born. She was 15 in human years and 101 in dog years. She was a great dog.

Her name was B.B. She was a playful dog. She liked to play with us when we were outside running around. She loved a little dog bone that we threw for her. She ran after balls but then dropped them before she got to us. She'd just come back and wait for another one. We always had fun with her. Me and her had a lot of good times. We would race each other around the house. We watched movies together. She was the greatest dog in the world.

Roderick W., II

Age 8, Saint Florian

You Gotta Jump

I like the waves and going to the deep end. The waves are very high and when the waves are very high you can drown but you gotta jump. I remember when I went fishing. My mom only caught seaweed. And my Uncle Billy put the bait on the pole and I put my line there and I got a fish.

I caught 16 fish.

Alena G.

Age 8, Saint Florian

I Was Raised By...

I was raised by my mom
that listens to R&B music
that loves me and gives me
ideas like when I didn't
know what to do with my picture.

She is a loving mom who
will care for you.
She gives me my favorite foods:
Pizza and Chinese food.
Even though she doesn't like them.

She always says to me, "How
was your day?" Or when I'm
in trouble, "Go think
about it." And
I do.

She goes and gets me every day
from camp around her work
schedule. I'm proud
of my mom; she is a nurse of
teens and kids at St. Vincent
Hospital.

The Great Coffeecake

When I went to Starbucks with my mom, I got coffeecake. It had cinnamon and vanilla cake, and my mom got tea and a scone. It tasted like SWEET GLORY and cinnamon and sweet, sweet, sweet vanilla cake, and it had crumbs of vanilla cake and crumbs of cinnamon. It was moist.

Amiia G.
Age 7, Saint Florian

Bear Boots

They looked like bear boots. They were warm in the winter when I was cold. They had a lot of fur. My cousin gave them to me when I turned 5. They were kind of big. Now they are too little. They make me run fast in the snow. My sister can wear them one day. They felt warm when my feet were cold.

I remember when me and my friend JoJo and I were in kindergarten and we were racing at school in the park.

I remember this because I was wearing my boots and she was wearing shoes. And after, we were tired, and we sat on the bench. And our other friend Jemiah came and sat with us. They are so special to me. First we clapped, then we played a game, and we step and give each other a hug.

***

The Loose Tooth

Yesterday I was eating a hamburger and then my tooth came out. And I told my mom and she was excited. At night I had a loose tooth and my mom tried to pull it out and she put a string on it and it came out. When I was eating the hamburger, I didn't feel it drop off and I was eating something hard and I thought it was a piece of the bread. And when I finished my hamburger I spit it out and saw it was my tooth.

Zack W-D.

Age 12, Saint Florian

Buffalo Wild Wings

My favorite meal is bbq wings and hot wings. My dad and I went to Buffalo Wild Wings to meet our cousins. We all ordered the same things: the bbq wings and hot wings. The dippings were ranch, BBQ, hot sauce. I ate slowly because I didn't want the food to not be all gone.

We had comfortable seats they were basically like couches. When we were all done we ordered a dessert brownie and ice cream. We finished and I was stuffed and my stomach was aching in pain. My dad told me to drink Sprite to see it if would work but it didn't.

When we went home I sat down and started playing video games until my stomach ache stopped.

***

The Day I Lost My Backpack

I was in the talent show and had forgotten a lot about it. 2 days later I just found out that I lost my backpack. I got so caught up that I forgot about it because the talent show was funny. I thought if I came back I could find it and get it but it was harder than I thought. My family was bugging me about the backpack for days. 4 days later I found it.

Ciaran McQuiston

Student Teacher, Concord & Saint Florian

"Look, I Wrote This!"

I never knew until this summer how much I loved working with children, despite the fact that I have two little sisters and babysit many evenings for the children in my neighborhood. This has been some of the most validating work I have ever done: helping somebody to write a story—no matter how mundane the subject matter—and having them really value my assistance and input gives me an overwhelming feeling of accomplishment. To be able to help someone to feel truly proud, help them create something they want more than anything to bring home to their mothers and fathers and say, "Look, I wrote this," is truly a privilege.

I especially love working with the youngest groups of children. I very much have looked forward to those mornings all summer; when they begin to file in wearing their baby blue shirts, looking for a place to sit near their friends, eyes meet and hugs happen. I have never felt so loved by people I know so little. I get to spend time with these very young boys and girls—who will, somehow, one day, be men and women—at a pivotal time in their lives, the time in which they begin to decide who they are going to be as individuals, who they are going to be in terms of others. This is still an even playing ground for them. They still have no verbal filter except that of their still-developing vocabulary.

There was one little boy in particular who always made my day. Every time I worked with his group, he begged me to come sit with him. Most days, I was not able to work with just him, as the group was always rather large and our numbers (the instructors, interns, and volunteers) were few in comparison. So on the days I would sit with others, working with them on their writing and listening to their lengthy explanations of this and that, this boy would come up to me with his writing and ask me to read it, tell him what I thought. His eagerness to have me see his work made me feel so special and proud. Here I was, your average Joe, suddenly swept into a world where kids wanted my advice, my validation. And as a result of their hard work and our subsequently positive exchanges, they left the room feeling accomplished.

Every time I work with these wonderful children at St. Florian, I cannot help but think, "these kids will grow up one day. They won't be kids forever." Although I am not spending a massive amount of time with them and they may not even know who I am a couple of years from now, I am satisfied—no, elated—to know that one day, these kids will have beautiful experiences and do amazing things... and I was able to be a small part of that journey.

Morgan W.

Age 9, Saint Florian

Raised By My Dad

I was raised by my dad.
I was raised by a problem
solver. I was raised by a kid
lover. I was raised by a movie
lover. I was raised by a ribs
lover. I was raised by a man
with great hearing.

I was raised by my dad. Every time
there was I problem he was
as fast as a cheetah to solve
it. I was raised by my dad.
Every time I was sad he
made me happy. I was raised
by my dad. Every time there was
a movie in the Redbox he liked
he would get it.

I was raised by my dad.
Every time he smelled
his dad's ribs he would run to
them. I was raised by my dad.
Every time he would hear somebody in pain he would run to them.

Rachel Johnson

Student Teacher, Saint Florian & La Plaza

Asking the Right Question

The summer of 2013 was not shaping up to be the summer I wanted it to be. It was going to be hard to live at home when I spent six weeks the previous summer studying abroad; packing a sixteen-week literature course into five weeks did not sound appealing; and all of my friends were leaving to take part in awesome activities around the world. To top it off, I had only been offered a volunteer position with the Indiana Writers Center Summer Youth programs, meaning I'd have to work the same part-time retail job I'd had since high school as well in order to save any money. Not sure of how much I should commit to, I created a schedule with the Writers Center that had me volunteering at both Saint Florian and La Plaza on Wednesdays.

On my first Wednesday at La Plaza, I sat at the back of the room between a boy and a girl. I didn't talk much to either of them beyond encouraging them to continue writing their lists even after they thought they were finished. At the end of our two-hour session, I watched the kids file out of the classroom, unsure of both their names and what my experience for the summer would hold.

A week later, we arranged the desks into islands for a group activity. As the kids shuffled in, I headed to a table with two boys, one that I vaguely recognized as the boy with whom I had worked the week before. Lowering myself into the seat across from him, Christian looked up and asked, "Hey, you weren't here on Monday. Where were you?"

I was a little taken aback that he had remembered me. "I'm only coming here on Wednesdays," I replied. "Is that alright?"

"Yeah, I guess," he said indifferently, turning to talk to the boy next to him.

Christian seemed to accept my explanation for why I was only there once a week, but I couldn't stop thinking about what he had asked me. While I had only been thinking of what it would cost me to work with the program, Christian was asking me to remember that the reason I signed up for the program in the first place was to advocate for the kids to share their stories in their composition books. By only working once a week, I was missing half of the prompts we asked the kids to write about, and I didn't get to reread their entries while transcribing their notebooks after each session. Christian's question hadn't been an accusation that I wasn't doing my job, but an invitation to do it with more of a purpose.

The following Monday, I showed up to La Plaza, half expecting Christian to notice as I sat down at his island that it was a Monday and I wasn't supposed to be there. When I started to get more involved, I was invited into the students' memories, invited to share in their ideas about the state of the world, invited to know them as real people. While more than once I left a session questioning my future as a high school English teacher and my abilities as a writer, I ultimately rediscovered the reason why I had truly decided to get involved with the Writers Center in the first place: with a pencil in hand and a notebook on the desk in front of them, these kids are seriously powerful.

This book is a physical collection of the invitation Christian extended to me. I'd like to extend that same invitation to you.

Angela H.
Age 13, Saint Florian

A Surprise Visitor

On Thursday June 27, 2013 at 3:00 pm. We had a surprise I kind of knew already. We were coming from Art with a Heart; we were going to the gym, and we saw her. As we were calling her name, she blended in. She had on a yellow shirt and she's short. She was walking towards the gym with a counselor. Kameelah called her name and she turned around. Her two favorite cadets ran up to her and gave her a big hug. Then we went outside to take some pictures. Before you knew it, it was time for the bus riders to leave. I was sad as I gave her the last hug before I left. We got on the bus, as the bus pulled off we was waving at her, then we were gone. I sat down in my seat and was very quiet. I was too sad to talk. As soon as I got home, I texted then my face lit up 'cuz I was happy I was talking to her. Other people were texting me but I didn't reply because I was too happy I was talking to her.

The surprise was my favorite counselor. Her name is NIKI!!!!

***

I Was Raised By...

I was raised by a goofy, build-me-up basketball playing, pony tail wearing, fruit snack, pop tart eating kind of woman.
A "Hey, girl, Hey" kind of woman.
Always showing teeth kind of woman.
A good, hugging everyone kind of woman.

Enas H.

Age 10, Saint Florian

Who Raised Me

I was raised by my parents who give me sweets on the weekend. Take me to Dave & Busters. Who give me cool shoes.

I was raised By a 5 foot 8 tall mom with auburn hair who always wears a suit when she teaches as a teacher. She is an Indian person from Wisconsin, She's a very hard worker and always has my back. My mom makes a bunch of Indian and American foods.

I was raised by a 5 foot 10 dad that is almost bald with black hair (don't ask me how I know that), who takes me places, works a lot, who brings be back souvenirs from whatever city he came back from, who gets me cool shoes, takes me out to dinner, and cooks. He plays a ton of sports and has taught me half the stuff I know. He has made me a baseball all-star. My dad is the lightning of my thunder.

I was raised by Renaissance man and an amazing woman.

***

Something Lost

I have lost many things but, the things I have lost the most are baseball games. I have lost probably about 50 baseball games, but on the bright side I've won more games than I've lost. I really don't like it when I lose and it puts me down for a while.

Taini H.

Age 13, La Plaza

T-a-i-n-i

My name is Taini. My name describes me. I am short and whenever people say my name, they always say, "Oh, Taini, because she's Tiny!" Most people think my name is spelled T-i-n-y but is actually is spelled T-a-i-n-i. I really like my name. It's unique. I have never heard of anyone else with this name. I would never change my name. I think this name is perfect. My name makes me think of my mom. The reason my name reminds me of her is because she is short like me. She's similar and that's it. She thought of my name. She came up with it. When I was born, I was very little and that's why my mom named me Taini. I was a premature baby. I don't really remember how much I weighed but I was really small. My name is fun to spell in cursive. I like writing my name over and over again.

***

My Blanket

I got my blanket when I was born. My dad got it for me. The nurse wrapped me in it. I still have it and I sleep with it. The blanket is pink and white. It has a carousel. My blanket reminds me of my dad when he is away or at work. Whenever I hold it, it feels like he is right next to me. My blanket is very soft and comfortable to sleep with. I love it.

***

I am like my blanket because I like being in warm places and feeling warm. I like riding carousels and I like the colors pink and white.

Lauren H.

Age 8, Saint Florian

Sacred Places

My sacred place is the mall. I love the mall. I go shopping almost every week. I love the mall. I always go. I like how it is inspiring and full of life. It is just so fun. I always go to Justice, The Mickey Mouse store, the pretzel store, and I go shopping. The mall is my House. And I always always always always buy toys and I always go with my Grandmother. It makes me feel good and happy. Shopping at the mall makes all of my worries go away. It smells like yummy pretzels and candy. The lights in the store are very bright and call me in.

***

My Mom

My mom is funny, happy, she is pretty, smart.
Wonderful. Her name is Pam Ann H.
She is short, with straight hair.
She cooks, cleans, and reads big books.
She loves to make macaroni
She works at the hospital to help people eat better.
Her clothes are pretty, with all kinds of items.
Her floral perfume makes me happy when I smell it.
We play tennis and go outside together.
She takes care of me when I'm sick.
She talks to me when I'm sad.
"Go to bed" she says.

Celeste W.

Volunteer, Saint Florian

I have no children.

But for a few, short weeks I borrow a few dozen of someone else's kids
Who vibrate, and wiggle,
And grin, and pout,
And laugh and cry,
And scribble and inscribe,
And refuse and accede...

...As we attempt to build a rainbow
From all of the colors they bring to us
In their tight, moist fists.

Outside the school walls
I hear echoes of 16-year-old boys being shot in the streets
And I try to avert my attention from news of a trial in Florida
As I help a boy with white teeth as big as Chiclets
Write about playing basketball with his big brother.

A little girl writes that her mother's favorite hue
Is the color yellow,
But that she loves the movie "The Color Purple."
That makes me smile,
Not only because of the child's expressive use of words,
But as I remember how wonderful it was for me to know
That a woman who looked like me
Wrote about other women

Who looked like me.

These children are brown and mocha
And tan and ebon,
And their hair is straight and curly
And kinky and braided
And twisted into baby dreads.
And I see my brother and my sister
And my cousins in their earnest, upturned faces.

"All eyes forward!"
They hear, but they still squirm with internal combustion
Like they have places to go. Right. Now.
I wonder what they see in front of them.

"Click!"
They respond reflexively as they have been taught.
I hope every time they say "Click!" a wheel in the universe
Turns in their favor;
I wish for these little rainbow-builders
That they will hold this world in their hands
And shape it, rather than it shape them.

I have no children.
But I hope they know
They have me.

Elijah H.

Age 9, Saint Florian

Surprise Gift

I remember when I was 5 and it was my mom's birthday. My cousin put me in a box. But I had my DS, so I would not get bored. Then he taped the box then put wrapping paper on it. He gave it to my mom, and then she opened it. I jumped out and said, "Happy Birthday!" She screamed for a shock.

***

Who Raised Me

I was raised by my grandma
She feeds me lasagna and sometimes desserts with a chocolate falling mountain
looking like candy bars of chocolate.
She gives me clothes. My favorite shirt is Naruto.
She takes care of me.
She loves me.
She pays for me.
I help raise my nephew Christian.
He is cute.
He talks.
He walks.
He plays.
He calls me Uncle Elijah.

Aylin J.

Age 14, La Plaza

I Am a Book

I am a book because I am filled with knowledge and adventure. I can take you places that are only described in your mind, that you are determined to create or imagine. I fill your head with knowledge and you are free to keep it or dump it. It could be filled with fantasy or with menial things you are determined to read. I can pick from technology or from pieces of paper. I can be the most wanted book or the fat dusty one sitting on the shelf. With more pages, more knowledge or adventure. Less pages, less knowledge. You are the one to choose, which I hope, to read. Either with a lot of pages or not. I can be for grown-ups or for small children. Sometimes I can make you feel feelings or knowledge. I can entertain you when you're bored or lonely. I can always be your second friend. I can give you lots of emotion if your favorite character dies. I'm just a book that wants to be opened and read.

***

My Mom, My Best Friend

The favorite person is my mom; she was always there for me. She's like a best friend. Even though she has my brother, she still makes time for me. She knows me so well. I know she'll always be there. I know how to convince her to buy my things. I think she's doing a good job of raising me. They've always taught me something new. My sister and my mother have been teaching me well.

Allen J., II

Age 12, Saint Florian

Remembering Florida

I remember the day of July 6, 2012 and it was sunny. Something made me feel good. Florida, one of the best places to hit the beach. The new suitcase pulled from the attic was blue and white. I pulled everything out of my drawers, and then I pulled 2 pairs of shoes and some sandals. Adidas, of course. I could smell the freshly cut grass and heard the birds chirping. I got in a truck and left for the airport. We checked our bags out and got on the plan. After checking into the hotel and putting our bags up and hitting the mall. I saw so many things.

***

A Very Loving Kind of Family

Some church-loving, fried-chicken-eating kind of folks. A Jamaican grandmother with a knack for cooking good food. Another grandmother from Kentucky with Southern accent and a love for everyone she knows. Aunts and Uncles from the east coast of the United States and others from Haughville and 9th street. Finally, a mother from Bayshore who loves playing and singing with a loud voice. Has 6 siblings and has a really nice fashion style and loves shows. Last but not least a father who's the first Allen Johnson. A football, basketball, and baseball watching man. An average man who works and has a 2012 Dodge Ram red truck. A man who loves me and our family. I was raised by a very loving kind of family.

Jordan J.

Age 9, Saint Florian

Collard Greens and PS3

I am raised by a New Yorker mom who is principal at school 65 who makes a lot of money each day and who loves me the most in the world. She cooks great collard greens. I am raised by a father who makes the best chili in the whole wide world, who plays with me, who listens to rap music and gospel, who loves me, who watches TV with me, like Sportscenter, and who wrestles with me. I'm raised by 3 older brothers and two sisters. When we play my PS3, I always lose because they are the Heat and I'm the Raptors, thank you! Yeah!

***

Basketball Brothers

I remember I had on Lebrons. I was at the basketball court with my three older brothers. It was two-on-two. It was me and Desean vs. Allen and Murice. I passed the ball to Desean and he dunked it on Murice, and he got angry!! So when he got the ball, he shot the ball, and I got angry, so when I got the ball, I dunked with my new Lebrons on Allen, so he got mad!! Allen dunked it so hard that the court broke and my shoes fell off, so we went to the park and had a race, and I won and then we went to the braids shop and got braids.

***

A special time is with my dad. We go shopping for food. When we get to the check out, he says, "You can get gum, Twix, Snickers, chips, and pop." We go home. We play basketball and he wins. I let him win. We play my PS3. We play 2K13. My dad is the Heat and I am the Knicks. My dad wins. We do this every day. I like to do this. It's FUN!

Zion J.

Age12, Saint Florian

I Remember...

I remember dunking on my friend Camryn.
I remember my first day of camp.
I remember when I won my first championship
I remember playing with my brothers when I was a kid.
I remember going to my first NBA game
I remember catching my first fish
I remember playing football with my friends in the street
I remember going to the New Yorker
I remember driving up to the pond
I remember hooking the fish
I remember reeling in the fish
I remember eating McDonald's on the way there

***

Lost: Realistic Fiction

It's an average sunny day, everything seems normal. My parents take me to the park. Everything is going great. Then something terrible happens... I don't see my parents. A million things are going through my mind. Did they abandon me? I got a clenching pain in my stomach. I can feel the tears developing in my eyes. I can see the sun slowly but steadily falling out of the sky. I feel like a fireball filling with the pressure of sadness, fear, and anger.

Collaborative

Concord

***

Summertime

When we lie by the pool in the sun,
we hear kids' screams
and the splashing of water
like snakes hissing, distant
blades cutting tall grass
and a dog barking endearingly
at its owner. As we absorb
the sun's heat, a sudden
splash of water
jars us from our comfort.

--Azhure S., Brianna D., Olivia G., Ciaran M., and Shari W.

***

Shari Wagner

Lead Instructor, Concord

Moments of Inspiration

Some of my favorite memories this summer were when my students at Concord experienced a sudden flash of inspiration—an "aha" moment that revealed how they could take a poetry assignment and forge something original and meaningful from it.

We were a small class, and since most of our meetings were held outdoors at Garfield Park or the Nina Mason Pulliam Ecolab at Marian University, this inspiration often occurred when we sat down to write at a picnic table or a bench. This was Azhure's second summer of workshops, and I enjoyed observing how quickly and intently she'd begin writing her poems. The mere meeting of pencil and paper seemed to bring inspiration, whether she was writing about golfing with her aunt or the origins of her name. For other students the moment of inspiration might be triggered by a list of questions, free writing or words of encouragement from our interns, Olivia and Ciaran, who were adept at fanning a hesitant spark into a flame. For Brianna, voicing her fear that she had nothing to write and then hearing our disbelief seemed to open the door to brilliant inspiration: her desired monument would be "a beaker of water;" her lobster claw plant persona would "dangle like a wind chime."

Sometimes a student found inspiration for a poem long before he or she hunkered down to write. When we were hiking through the Ecolab, I noticed Juan's curiosity about a well that is supposedly haunted; his intense focus was the kind of honing in that catches the faint drip of water . . . the old bricks . . . the grayness of stone. On that same trip, I was also pretty sure what Malaki would write about. He was keenly alert as he spied a turtle sunning itself on a log in the lake, so attentive that he would later write that its yellowish green was the color of spinach, its tail "got straight super straight" when it jumped into the water and its face looked out "like the end of a pencil when you write." A writer must be poised to receive messages from the universe—like Jalen S. when he bent down near the large koi at the Garfield Conservatory pond. This shimmering, speckled fish rose partly out of the water, moving its mouth, Jalen noted, as if hungry or struggling to speak. Jasmine had a mission as soon as I mentioned the possibility that the conservatory might harbor her namesake flower. She had never smelled or seen a picture of jasmine, so finding one became a quest rewarded by creamy flowers she described as having "a hint of vanilla" and glossy leaves that "scrunch / up as if they were doing / sit ups." This plant appeared in Jasmine's next poem, too, when she envisioned it growing around a statue symbolic of herself.

Sometimes students were inspired to turn an assignment on its head. Jalen R. S. didn't see the sense in writing a poem in which he imagined himself speaking as a favorite animal or plant. He could have rebelled by not writing but, instead, created a wonderful poem mentioning the conservatory's "sticky blue flowers" and the "rubbery texture of koi." He asserted that he loved the koi and that he smelled like the trees, yet he returned to the resounding chorus, "I am me." Jalen was doing what poets do: changing expectations, pushing boundaries, rewriting the assignment.

My "aha" moment is coming now as I compose this reflection. A spark occurs when one surface strikes another. The sparks of inspiration I observed this summer usually appeared when students found a strong connection, a sudden bond to something or someone else: a special golfing partner, a namesake flower, a favorite animal or a mysterious place. Brianna's Whitmanesque "yeah, that is me" at the end of her persona poem has been the motivational force of poets throughout history. Personal memory and experience are the materials poets use, but empathy is that force that forges them into art. Nikki Giovanni, a poet whom Azhure Giovanni S. was named for, makes a similar claim. "I want to be clear about this," she writes. "If you wrote from experience, you'd get maybe one book, maybe three poems. Writers write from empathy."

Elexsis J.

Age 13, Saint Florian

I Remember...

I Remember when I was young and pretty
I Remember when I got smart for the first time
I Remember when I couldn't write my name
I Remember when I started first grade
I Remember when I turned 11!
I Remember when I ate a whole Big Mac
I Remember the first Day of School
I Remember when I had to do the dishes
I Remember the first time I fell off the bike
I Remember the first day I got kicked out of school

I Remember when I used to say I wouldn't eat a Big Mac.
I Remember I was happy because I was getting a Big Mac
I Remember me tearing the box open
I Remember that was the first time putting my phone down for more than a 5 min
I Remember when I did not want to stop.

***

Losing My Everything

I remember when I lost the one I love. They were my everything. They were there when I cried when I got in trouble. I don't want to lose the one I lost again. People are here for a reason. They were there when I needed food and a place to sleep. I lost the someone that cared about me when they were not even thought of. They're still here, right by my side, but she's in her soul.

GenNevion J.

Age 10, Saint Florian

Houses

I liked the houses. I wanted to live in them.
They looked white.
They made me feel...far away from home.
I liked their T.V.'s.
I met a friend. He was a boy. We played
everything on Xbox.

Jaime J.
Age 10, Saint Florian

Who Raised Me

I was raised by a woman who is nice, funny, light caramel, brown eyes, beautiful and intelligent. I was raised by a woman who loves to cook and sing to the Lord every Sunday morning. I was raised by a woman who says, "Get your homework done." I was raised by a woman who loves to eat potatoes and fried chicken. I was raised by a woman who loves the color yellow, but loves the movie The Color Purple. I was raised by a woman who loves me so. I was raised by my mom, whom I love.

***

Marcia's Lunch

I remember my grandma made her famous lunch. She called it "Marcia's Lunch." It had Ritz crackers, turkey meat, sliced cheese, and, finally, Lay's chips. It was good, but then I saw a piece of hair on the cheese. So then I thought, "I'm not going to eat that." But then I thought again, "Isn't this just a Lunchable, but just chips and no Oreos?"

***

Converse Everywhere

I have a pair of shoes I just love. They are Converse. They are black because black goes with everything with a little bit of white, and on the very back of my heel it says "All STAR." These shoes are very comfortable. They feel like I am in the warm and soft sand at the beach. They smelled like sweet candy. I remember that before my uncle died, he gave me these shoes. These shoes really mean a lot to me.

Jimmesia J.

Age 13, Saint Florian

***

I Remember...

I remember hitting her
I remember she was on crutches
I remember it took place in the cry room
I remember I was doing homework at the time
I remember I had to go down to the office
I remember she got in my face
I remember they started the argument
I remember my friend trying to leave
I remember two girls going to tell
I remember she not getting in trouble
I remember having a dream about her
I remember she was tortured in this dream
I remember she didn't talk to me anymore

***

Collaborative

Concord

The Statue of Major General Lawton Speaks
Garfield Park, Indianapolis

What am I doing here?
Am I famous or something?
Why can't I move?
Why am I still in this uniform?
Why do I have no color but gray
like an old TV screen?
Why am I so serious,
looking down
and posed like I'm in a picture
of a war
while I'm in this park?
And what's that behind me?
Is it a meteor
or my knapsack?
Can I go back to sleep?
My legs hurt.

--Azhure S., Brianna D., Jalen S., Juan A., Jasmine A., and Jalen St.

Ja'Len K.

Age 7, Saint Florian

Eating Oranges

oranges are
fun to open
you need
to peel
it and then
you eat
it. It is salty
and sweet.

***

I Remember...

When I got an Xbox 360. It was black and it had this little camera on it. And it got stolen. And then my daddy had got me another one for Christmas. I played sonic and football, basketball and tennis. I played the racing game. I almost crashed, I was real close to a car, but then I had played a superhero game, Batman, the Joker, and Superman. It had a lot of people. I played it at my house. I played soccer and boxing. I felt happy.

Fredy J-C.
Age 13, La Plaza

My Human Rights and My Words

The things I own right now since the government began to be corrupt are my human rights and my words. The government cannot violate my human rights by spying, looking, or reading my text messages. They also don't hear my words or others, and that violates the Bill of Rights created by our founding Fathers. Is this how the govt. violates the things I own?

Since I got mad over what the govt. did, I decided to help myself so I decided to be a lawyer and work up the ladder.

I will do my best and work through the challenges and make true justice. I want to be the next John F. Kennedy or Abraham Lincoln.

The government is acting like a lion
Human rights is being a free deer

***

The Heart of My Name

For me, my name is truthful and wise. Truthful to me means me being honest and speaking about it. Wise is when I have to take a decision to make a good choice.

The negative thing about me is that sometimes I would be sad. Sadness mostly brings me down and makes me feel like I'm in a dark place.

Mar'Kayla K.

Age 9, Saint Florian

Like Coco Butter

I was raised by a loving, sweet, and caring mom. I was raised by a big heart woman and a calm loveable mom. She is like coco butter. Her name is Nichole McClung. She taught me how to do lots of things. My mom is like a sister to me, I am raised by Justice and Clareis. My mom taught me how to almost do everything. I am raised by one person, maybe two. My dad and my mom.

***

My Bed

My sacred place is my bed. The warm and soft cover with the fluffy pillows. It is sacred because I could be there all day and it's very comfortable. My cover is soft like the clouds and blue like the sky and furry like a dog and it's light blue. My pillow has polka dots on one side and stripes on the other, it's very colorful. I have another cover and it's kind of like a quilt, it's purple and blue. My bed is big and it's only meant for one person.

Two days ago I remember when I was tight, warm, cozy and a soft feeling in my bed. Sometimes I would move around a lot to get more comfortable, I would move all the ways to get in a spot, and this all was when I was going to bed. I had a hard and playful day that day, and also my cover has polka dots on one side and stripes on the other like my pillow. It smells like coco butter on me after I get out the shower. It sounds like my TV in my room with the voice of a little boy on *Home Alone 3* and the rumbling when I move around. It's important to me because I can get lots of sleep and not be tired in the morning. I got my soft and furry cover from Wal-Mart and my pillowcases and big cover from Christmas. My mom bought it for me.

Malaki L.
Age 11, Concord

Little Turtles

A turtle on a log with his little head
with a yellowish green color like fresh spinach.

When it jumped into the water it sounded like me dropping ice into a cup of
water.

When he jumped his little toes popped out and his tail got straight. Super straight.

The shell was very textural
like stars in the sky put together.

When he showed his face, it poked out like the end of a pencil when you write.

Noah M.

Age 11, Saint Florian

IHOP French Toast and Love

I had French toast from IHOP. It was really good. It had strawberries, blueberries and a lot of syrup. I Love going to IHOP. It is my favorite breakfast place.

I was so hungry that morning. I knew what I wanted before I got there. French toast is the best breakfast in the world. I love it.

Next time I am going to try a different type of French toast. I think I will love that.

I was with my family and they did not try it but they loved what they had. I remember putting so much syrup my mom said, "Stop." I love putting syrup on my breakfast food. Including different flavors of syrup.

***

We Were So Confident

I remember I lost the championship in basketball. We were the Bucks and we played the Pistons. We were 13-0 coming in to the Championship. We lost 17-21. I was very sad we finished the season 13-1. We got the runner-up second place trophy. The other team got a big trophy. I was a forward on the team; I got six points in the game. We were so confident. We thought we were going to win. I might have been a little cocky. I learned not to be as cocky. We were at FJH. It was two years ago in January. Hopefully we will win it next year.

66

Christopher M.

Age 9, Saint Florian

I Feel Like a King

My mom cooking my favorite chicken, which are buffalo chicken wings. We eat them with corn on the cob, green beans, baked beans, and corn bread. Drink it with lemonade and we eat it at the kitchen table. My mom cooks it in the morning but we have to wait until dinnertime to eat. One time, she cooked me 30, and I put some of them in my lunch box and I ate them for lunch the next day. After we eat the buffalo wings, we eat brownies. Sometimes I put ice cream on my brownies. When I eat chicken wings I feel like a king. I have chocolate chip brownies I feel like a king because I feel in my comfort zone eating.

***

I am Being Raised by Mom and Dad

My mom: she cooks for me. She taught me how to do the dishes. She taught me how to wash clothes. She helps me with my homework after school. She taught me how to cook.

My dad taught me how to cut grass. Taught me how to weed eat, how to put more string in the weed eater. He taught me how to use a blower. He taught me how to manage my money. My dad's going to teach me how to open a bank account. He plays video games with me. I play basketball with him. He taught me how to play basketball. He taught me how to come in the house without him being there. He plays remote-control trucks with me. He taught me how to clean the shower. And he taught me how to change a light bulb.

Leeann Sausser

Student Teacher, Saint Florian

"What Happens If We Don't Write?"

Sitting at a table of three very over-excited seven-year-olds is a daunting task, especially when you have one on your left, one on your right, and one in front of you. There's no escaping. They have lots to say and no idea of when to stop. That day I had already learned about a trip to New York City, the best place to get tacos (Taco Bell), the probability of one girl getting a dog, and how one kid wouldn't keep his shirt tucked in.

Oh, and of course who raised them, the actual writing prompt of the day.

Getting the kids to focus on that topic was quite the challenge. I tried using their name tags as "invisible barriers," making it a game to see who could write the most, and simply asking non-stop questions until they would write down something just so I would focus my attention on the next unwilling writer.

Finally the girl on my right looked up and asked:

"What happens if we don't write? What's our punishment?"

Uh…

Well, nothing. We could always tell the counselors they were not listening or following directions. But I would feel guilty punishing a kid who just didn't feel like writing that day. There are lots of days I don't feel like writing, and nothing happens to me.

Miraculously, an answer came into my head.

"I will be very, very disappointed in you," I said.

The gasps of little children are the funniest things. Their eyes widen like my cat when she is begging for turkey lunch meat and the little bubble of air they inhale sounds more like a hiccup than a shocked gasp. But when they do it all at once, you know it's serious.

This choir of inhaling sounded too serious. So I quickly followed up with an explanation for them.

"If you don't write, I'll be disappointed that I can't read your stories" I said. "I love to read what you write each week."

Faster than they could eat the tacos they loved, three little heads bent down and scribbled. For the two minutes before distraction hit them, I could enjoy the sound of pencils dancing along their paper partners.

The stories little kids tell you don't always make sense and they don't always sound true. Too often, these jumbled tales become background noise to the older people around and the kids' childhood musings are lost. So when children are given permission to tell their stories, to say all they want, they want to tell everything. When you are six or seven, your hand does not let you speak as quickly as your mouth, so you gravitate toward speaking your stories first, writing them down second.

When that little girl asked me, "What happens if we don't write?" my first thought was "nothing." But that couldn't be farther from the truth. If the youth of our world don't write, we lose their voice. It's a voice that may include run-on sentences, disorganized thoughts, and simple words, but it is a precious voice that sounds out the song of childhood, as captured by children.

This is the singing voice that I heard every week at Saint Florian. May it now be the singing voice you read in the pages of this book.

William M.

Age 11, Saint Florian

Like Epic Clouds

My adventure with my black, blue, and green Adidas was epic. These shoes are big and comfortable. They have a dirt stain on them but I don't know how they got that way. When I went to Holiday World I rode the Raven, the Legend, and the Voyage with my shoes, but that is not the epic part. The epic part is that I was running toward the pool but I forgot to take my shoes off. I jumped up and out of my shoes and I thought my shoes were goners, but I flipped into the pool and caught them. I ran track with my shoes and won, but the cool part about the shoes are that I am wearing them right now. My shoes are not old or new they are in their toddler years because they are 2 years old. When I wear them they feel like clouds.

***

Cobbler and Cookies

I lost my grandma to colon cancer. She was a teacher. She taught my uncle when he was in kindergarten. My Grandma was a strict teacher, if she heard that any of her children were bad you would have a very strict punishment. My Grandma was a great cook. She made everything from scratch. My mom said she made the best peach cobbler and cookies. I heard stories about my grandma that she would never be able to see her grandkids. I found a little piece of my Grandma. I found her cobbler and cookies.

Kaleb K.

Age 7, Saint Florian

Always Upstairs

I was raised by my mom. I looked like my little brother. I was raised in Mississippi. It was Hurricane Sandy. We moved to Indiana when I was about 1 or 2. My dad, Aunt, and family was there to see my mom give birth. They hug me sometimes when I'm at my dad's house. I Skype my mom and my auntie and my Dad is always upstairs. My dad used to play soccer and it makes me want to play soccer. I still have his trophy in my new house. I put it somewhere no one can find it.

When I was about 4 years old, I used to have a sty, so I got this medicine and put it in my eye. My mom used 7Up and crackers when I'm sick. She plays cards with me. We play trash.

My dad lets me get a lot of snacks. I get one in the morning, after lunch, and after dinner. She cooks everything. She runs a day care. My mom gave me a job at a day care.

***

A Dog That Barks

My favorite toy is a dog that barks a lot. It's in my mom's trunk. It has red and white clothes and a hat. It got on my mom's nerves because it kept barking. I got it from Burger King. I miss playing with the toys. I play with the toy in the living room. It was fun. It's about this big.

Anthony M.

Age 13, La Plaza

After Death

I know people believe in heaven and hell but what if there isn't? Supposedly before you die you get flash backs of your whole life. From baby to whatever you are now. Just seeing how much you changed. How much people actually looked at you. Maybe Heaven and Hell is just a dream zone or an Imagination place that you got taught to believe. What happens to the people who don't believe in it? Do you just live in your mind in the coffin you got chosen to be in? Maybe you dream for your life or you live on in a world where no one can see you.

What <u>really</u> happens before and after you die?

***

Deep Down

Deep down I really want to say that I dislike a lot of people and they don't know it. Also deep down I want to say that I'm stronger than what people think I am. Most people don't know how my life is. And what happened in it. If I could I would tell everyone how my life is.

Deep down I really want to say that I get bullied a lot in regular school. That's why I'm the way I am. That's why when people mess with me the anger and hate that build up has to come out. I already met my limit. I hope it doesn't happen again. You might ask how I got bullied. I was physically bullied and verbally bullied. Over and over again every day of that year.

Bryce M.
Age 7, Saint Florian

Ten Feet Tall

I was raised by a granddad who buys powdered donuts for me and my brother. My Granddad lives in Georgia. My granddad comes to my house and spends the night then he takes us to Georgia. He is ten feet tall.

I PLAY WITH HIS DOG!

***

I Remember...

I had a racecar. It was orange and red. My dad gave it to me. I played with it at home. I was racing it against my brother's car. His was blue and orange. We raced them on the kitchen floor. My brother usually won. I told him, "Can we keep on racing again?" He said, "We can."

***

My mom gave me a toy train. It was blue. When I had it I was happy.

Elyjah M.

Age 8, Saint Florian

Cool New Shoes

I was at the barber shop and my mom said, "I got you some new cool shoes." I got really excited and disturbed my barber. I asked my mom if I could get them after my haircut. When my haircut was over I got off my chair and ran to my mom's car as the oxygen hit me. When I got to the front seat I saw the box and I opened the door. As I grabbed the box I opened the box and I couldn't believe what I saw, then I saw my mother coming and asked her, "Were these the ones you got me?" Then the words that came out of her mouth were, "Yep." I got really excited and put them on faster than any other shoes I've ever put on.

***

She Says I'm Truthful

I was raised by my great, great, grandmother, Sally Hester. She works with the Saint Florian Center. She says I'm truthful. Anytime somebody is crying she goes over and helps them out. She also plays the piano really well. She wipes my tears off of my face. She warms me up with her cuddles. She reminds me of my family. She is nice and sweet, sweeter than honey.

Stephanie M.

Age 11, Saint Florian

Spoiled

I was raised by family. By mom and dad, Aunts and Uncles, by cousins, and grandparents. I was raised by an artistic mom. A mom who hates to hear me cry. A mom who tries to understand every time. I was raised by a fun-filled dad. A dad who got me out there. A dad who spoils me until I burst. I was raised by supporting aunts and uncles. Aunts and Uncles who love me. I was raised by cousins – Cousins who make me laugh. Cousins who love me even if we fight. I was raised by even more spoiling grandparents. Grandparents who loved me to the end. I was raised by a loving, helpful, supporting FAMILY! ☺

***

Shoes Under the Bed

These Pink and Black Nikes were one of my favorites. When I first saw these shoes I was in love. When me and my dad went to go visit my Grandmaw my aunt was also there. She told me she had got me a present. She said that they were upstairs in the bedroom. I ran upstairs wondering what the present was. When I got to the bedroom, she had a note on the door that said, "You have to find it." I looked everywhere: behind the door, under the covers, in drawers, behind pillows, in the closet, and the dresser. Then I finally looked under the bed. When I saw the box, I ripped it open and just stared. I ran downstairs with them on. All my dad could say was, "Oh no" because he knew and was right that I would wear them everywhere. Now they are two small but every now and then I squeeze my feet in those comfortable but tight shoes when we go on short trips like to the store. I love those pink and black Nike Air Max tennis shoes.

Andrew M.

Age 12, La Plaza

Rock on the Floor of the Ocean

"I wanted to swim farther in the deep," I said to myself as I saw the ocean in front of me. The day was perfect. Today was the day I swim farther, nothing is going to stop me. I dived into the water. It was cold and clear but okay. I swam fast to my father, he was on the other side. I swam until the point where I couldn't feel the floor of the ocean. I went down to the depth of the ocean. It felt as if I was a rock that's just going down to the bottom.

***

Bearded Women

I talk about a bearded women and how bearded women are cool. It is interesting to see a woman with a beard. I mean, come on, whoever is reading this, it is interesting. Admit it. OK 'nuff said. Back to the reason why I made this story. It tells me that if men are bearded so can women.

Whatever the man can do so can the women.

***

All-Night Diners

Yesterday I stayed at Denny at 1:08 am. I ate a cheeseburger and grapes. I was with my parents. I mean 1:00 in the morning I never want to stay there 'til that late. But anyway the cheeseburger was good I found a unique taste to it. My mind told me to go rest but I said "Later." Then it turned to 12:00 at night then my body asked again, "Go to sleep, man," and then I told my body, "5 more minutes." Seconds turned into minutes and then turned to hours. It was 1:00 a.m. Then my parents said we could go home. It was a relief to get out of that place. My mind told me to go and rest instead of staying at this restaurant.

Noemi M.
Age 13, Saint Florian

Going to the River

I remember when I went to the river in Mexico. We went walking to it. When we got there it was beautiful. You could hear the sound of the waterfall. I was young. I was like 4 or 5, I don't remember. They were getting in the river. I got in the river; it was cold. There were a lot of rocks so it was kinda hard to walk in it, but I didn't want to get in, only my feet, because I was scared the water was gonna take me away. But it was a great experience.

***

My Necklace

So my grandma gave my mom a bunch of necklaces and bracelets and rings before she left Mexico. When I got older I wanted a necklace just like my mom. My mom had a lot, so she gave me one. It had one heart on it, and I have another one on it and I just added the Hello Kitty thing on it. I've had it for years already.

***

I am a necklace.
I am important.
I have a heart of gold.
I am valuable.

Brett Hiatt

Student Teacher, Saint Florian & La Plaza

As It Is

We ain't speaking in no academia.
We ain't autotuning this art to articulate
flawed phrases into bubblegum band harmony.
We don't Photoshop the finger
from the corner of an otherwise
possibly perfect picture.

We tell it as it is.

Sit on the couch, we want to tell you
about buying mouthwatering cotton candy with dad,
playing videogames in the living room with mom,
driveway basketball with brothers and sisters,
getting smoked in the head with a rock,
grandma dying in her bedroom from cancer,
that sweet pair of kicks we wear only on special occasions.
That real stuff that happens
when you're young and tells more stories
than your television set ever could, recycling the same
formulaic, laugh track, sitcoms season after season.

We tell it as it is.

We are the street art under the bridge that says,
"I'm beautiful."
We are "excellent," inspiring an earthquake
of inspiration to crumble your structural
ideas of what true art is and why we're not.

We are the banned books tossed aside
for no better reason other than the simple fact:
That we are voice.
We are direct mirrors of society,
our community.
We are words that flow unfiltered
from the gritty ground floor of our soul,
of our neighborhood's soul.
We are culture.

And we tell it as it is.

We don't take our smiles for granted.
We've lost shoes, shattered iPhone screens,
got dunked on in 2k13, wanted to dye our hair
any color but green.
We are a community of funspiring
little champions.
We let the ink pump from our hearts
right out to the page to outright
out write any stuffy scholar who writes.
Out with the head. Gee wiz.
Listen, my friend, because

We tell it as it is.

LaNiyah P.
Age 6, Saint Florian

I Remember

I remember when I was two years old.

I remember I had a birthday cake. It was good. And I ate it with my fingers and my face was messy. It was delicious. I put my face in the cake. My face in the cake was fun. I felt happy like a beautiful day. My mommy my cousin and my bubby and my sissy Jayla were there. I wore a bib. We were at Chuck E. Cheese.

I remember I was a baby. I cried for my bottle. I don't know why I cried. I was happy. Bottle and my brother was the only thing I loved as a baby. I loved the baby milk.

***

A Lot of Love

I was raised. . . my mom and I had a closet full of clothes. She helps me read, she reads me stories. She cooks bratwurst for me. She makes noodle soup. She loves swimming with me and she teaches me how to swim. My mommy's rich but she's not. She has money, not that much. She has a lot of perfume, a lot of love from me.

She feeds me when I was a baby.

Joshua P.

Age 12, Saint Florian

Practice and Believe

Once I tried out for a basketball team. As the basket in front of me from the three point line-I miss, second shot- I miss, a three pointer, third-I concentrated. I looked to my left: family chanting. To my right: some teammates. Behind me: other team. In front: basket. I close my eyes and I shoot. I score. But I did not get the team because I missed the first two shots. After I went home, I exercised then went in our basement, did some weights, got a basketball, went outside, we had a basketball court. Shot half-court, it went in, kept shooting three pointers, all went in. Free throws, as well, went in. I was proud I made all those shots. Always practice for the rest of my life. I will always practice and believe.

***

Who Raised Me

I was raised by my mom; we both have things in common. We like food and trying new things. I LOVE my mom. She's Black. I'M mixed. She's nice and smart, caring and loving. My mom's five-five. I am too. My mom and I like shopping. I do too, plus drawing. She has no bad side. We go to Phillip's Temple C.M.E. Church. Dayron, Brandon, and Ms. go to my church.

Eric P.

Age 8, Saint Florian

Explore

I was raised by my dad and he always takes care of me just like my mom and she buys a house for my brother and my big sister and my dad teaches me how to make stuff and my mom teach me how to explore around the world and I told my mom when I grow up I want to explore around the United States.

***

Shark

It was a hot sunny day down by the river. My grandpa and I were ready for fishing, swinging around sea stars to attract fish and sharks. My small silver and black fishing pole held a blue glow in the dark sea star. Suddenly something cause my fishing line to jerk. I hold the twister and I saw a shark and I was happy that I got a shark and went home.

***

Food

I remember my favorite food and it's hot and it was spicy chicken and I remember breakfast. My favorite was waffles and pancakes I remember last summer last camp me and all the JCs went to breakfast. Me and Elyjah got chocolate strawberries and I like tacos and nachos and pizza and French fries and I like cake, donuts, cinnamon rolls, and fish, meatballs, and McDonalds, Burger King, and ribs. And candy.

Julianna Thibodeaux

Lead Instructor, Saint Florian

On my first day back working with the kids at St. Florian this year, I couldn't wait to see how the kids had grown. As soon as those familiar yellow and blue shirts came filing into their respective classrooms from the stairwell, I started to recognize them—many whose writing I had the privilege of shepherding as an instructor a year ago.

As our faces began to light up in mutual recognition, I began to recall the writing we had done together last summer. I imagined how another year had shaped their lives: what new experiences had molded their growing selves. What they had come to see, feel and love? What senses had been awakened in the course of their days?

As I watch my own children grow—they are now 18, 8, and 6—the years seem to truncate: each one becoming more compact and dense with the seemingly faster passage of time.

But as a child, the days seemed more like a lazy river: each one a slow succession of minutes floating toward the next meal, dismissal bell, play date, or trip to Minnesota to visit my grandparents. As I've watched the days pass through the eyes of an adult—as a parent responsible for the well-being of children, not just my own but those with whom I spend time as an aunt, a volunteer at my children's schools, a Girl Scout troop leader, or as an instructor in the Build a Rainbow program—those days seem to rush by with the momentum of a waterfall.

When I visited Niagara Falls for the first time, as a child, it seemed a monumental thing: a skyscraper of moving water. The immensity of it was almost too much to comprehend: the thick cascade creating an illusion of solidness, exploding into a translucent, light-filled spray at the bottom. When I made that same trip decades later, with two of my own children (the third was not yet born), I had the same sensation: I was silenced by the falls' powerful beauty, the same white wall of moving water creating an illusion of stillness.

But unlike when I was a child, as an adult, I looked at it as both a thing to be revered and as a thing fraught with real dangers—and so I backed away from the edge, sweat beading on my forehead, reaching back to assure myself that my then 1-year-old daughter was secure in her carrier.

And I realize now, looking back, that this is a perfect metaphor—not just for the passage of time but for how we write as adults. We have lived and experienced both joys and sorrows, and as we write about these moments in our lives—if anyone asks us to do so, or we are moved from within—then it is inevitable that those steps away from the edge, where we look upon our life as a series of moments rushing by, are initially measured. We know the dangers. But if we begin this process as children, then maybe we won't be afraid or overwhelmed by the rush of memory that will inevitably greet us as we grow older.

During my own childhood, those occasions to synthesize my experiences were few: creative writing was not regularly taught in school, and if we did write in the classroom—unless it was a research paper, comprehension exercise, or grammar assignment—it was of the "what I did on my summer vacation" variety. But even those seemingly more creative endeavors came back red-lined with corrections, making me ever more cautious the next time I was assigned a "creative" writing exercise.

One of the things I love about working with the kids at St. Florian is that I can imagine myself in their shoes: having the opportunity to express myself without the censure of an adult, but instead, the encouragement of both adults and peers. That's not to say that through the process of writing and with reader's questions they can't become better writers, because they can, and do: it's just that their writings won't be returned scarred with corrections. Instead, if they choose, their writing will be read aloud, and their peers will draw them out even more. And in many cases, their words will be made permanent in these pages.

The things they are writing about now will inevitably be viewed through a different sort of lens as they grow older: so that when Trinity writes as a 6-year-old about a dog she once had, with one of our interns helping to write down her emergent-writer words, the next year, or even two, she will write about that dog from a different perspective; moving her closer to understanding her need to feel secure in the world, or the importance of loving and being loved unconditionally.

Whether the kids write about favorite toys, pets, foods, trips, places or people, as they grow older and are encouraged to write at all—outside of English composition rubrics—they will have the opportunity to further synthesize the experiences of their lives, and understand that they meant something then—and they mean something now. Whenever that "now" is.

Amani M.

Age 13, Saint Florian

Food

To start off a cold food
being stored in a freezer
waiting for the moment to be heated.
To be sautéed or powdered with flour.
This food has the most power.
To be laid in a skillet and browned deep
or to swim in oil to be fried asleep
A one in a kind food.
When the human picks up its juicy goodness
It has no conscience, it's lost in heaven
dreaming above not knowing what's coming
till BOOOM. there you have it. The next thing
ya know your taste buds explode in
happiness knowing that you're the awesomest person they could have.
They rejoice in you and
make you feel new. If to only believe that it was to start off a
chicken.

**

Outside the Foggy Window

There lies grass drizzled in rain
The window paved with drops of tears
The splashing sound pierced my ears
This window seat
This foggy window
This note book
This pen
All sit here and wonder about themselves
When will I fall when will I dry when
Will I drown when will I try to become
Me again they to be whole this foggy window
paved with drops of tears
Waiting for its bright years.

Breanna N.

Age 12, Saint Florian

I was raised by...
Juicy, crispy, fried chicken
Going to the mall kinda
family. braiding hair tight
hands full of gel kinda
family spades playin gum
poppin kinda family barbeques
every week end, non-crying
very strong kinda family.
lip gloss, shoes, jewelry kinda
family. Neat hand writing
funny talking kinda family
very supporting, keeping me
on my toes kinda family.
A very hard working
kinda family.
***

iPod

I don't want to lose
My iPod 5th generation

It's green with engrave-
ment on it. It's engraved with
Happy 12th birthday Breanna L. N.

It has a clear case
on it but it has duct tape

My iPod has close
to fifty apps on it.

My mom will kill me if I lose it.

Skylar B.

Age 7, Saint Florian

My Doll

My favorite toy to play with is my doll. My doll is very special. I got it in Chicago. My mom bought it for me. It has long black hair, brown eyes, a pink shirt, a gray skirt with a pink belt and brown boots with a green butterfly. She is really special and I don't care if she's old because I still love her even though I train with it so when I grow up I'll know how to be a wife and mother. At Mel's, my friend, house I play with her and I play with it outside. One time I played with her outside. My sister told Mel to bring her doll outside with her so we could play with it. My doll smells like strawberries because she's sweet like strawberries. My doll's name is Rachel. My dad had to work in Chicago for a business trip. For two days I stayed there. My friend has one too so I will always keep it in mind.
The End!

***

The Taco

My taco was crunchy, and soft. Inside my taco was, meat, ranch and crunchy, and cheesy. The people with me were my two cousins, my sister, and my mom. I was at Taco Bell. I felt excited when I ate the taco. My mom bought them for me.
The End!

Will Lagunas

Volunteer, Saint Florian

It is difficult for me to express my experience at St. Florian in writing. I can really only say that I learned a great deal about the young minds that attend the program and that I deeply respect their ability to generate such great writing at such young ages. Those young minds helped me grow as a person through their optimism and charisma. Those little adults helped generate memories that have become embedded into my heart, overtaking previously treasured experiences.

At St. Florian I learned that a simple, unexpected hug can break even the strongest of men. That a true breathtaking moment is when a struggling child powers through his disability to share his own words with his peers and prove he can overcome. That sometimes all a child wants is someone who will listen, truly listen to their experiences and opinions. I have built close bonds with a number of these little adults and it is difficult to believe, but they have impacted my life far more than I have theirs.

I now know why people dedicate their time and efforts to develop programs like the Indiana Writers Center. It isn't to boost their own egos, or to create a program in order to seek personal gain. It is simply to create inspiring, positive, fun-filled moments that will impact the children's lives. Everything else that comes of it is a bonus. All-in-all I will treasure my memories from this summer and urge everyone to listen to the stories these children treasure and want to share

Aaron B-C.
Age 14, La Plaza

Look, Son

She said, "Look son, I don't like the things you do. I don't wanna go to the police station to pick up my 13 year old son." And she started crying and that's what made me change and make that promise. When I saw her cry the skies turned dark and that's when tears came out her eyes and made a hole in my heart and it made me make a promise to make her the proudest mother ever. And now I'm doing better in school, staying out of trouble, and making something of myself to make her proud of me. And never make my mom cry another tear over me. Because my mom is my whole world.

***

Wanna Get a Job

I wanna get a job because I can get money for myself and get my own money. And buy my own clothes. And get the things I wanna get not what my parents want me to get. And so I can put gas in my car. I don't think my Dad is gonna give me money for gas. And I also wanna get money so I can go out on road trips and take my girlfriend out to eat to a nice place.

Sydney Bl.

Age 9, Saint Florian

By a Woman

I was raised by a woman
named Linda B. who
get what I need: candy,
paper, coloring books, TV,
a phone, and iPad.
She makes my favorite
cake, chocolate cake.
When I'm having a bad day,
she says don't worry, and she
lets me play in her shoes
I was raised by a woman
named Linda B,
a woman that goes to
the store for people who
are sick. A woman who babysits
the neighbors' kids
so they can run errands,
and cares for me every day
and feeds me, takes me to McDonalds
3 days a week and that's why I love
her so much and my whole
family loves me so much and
cares for me and my mom
and dad teach.

91

Darolyn "Lyn" Jones

Lead Instructor, Saint Florian

"Thank you, Gregory"

We unschool the schooled, teach them that it's okay to —in fact— preferred to use "I," to write from their guts and not their heads, to not worry about spelling and grammar, but to get the words out and onto paper. I say this as someone who has been teaching kids to write both in and out of school for 22 years, but who has been writing since she could hold a pencil.

When I teach memoir writing, I share the following metaphor. A written memoir can be viewed as a photograph, waiting to be set up, taken, and developed so that it will most closely illustrate what the photographer saw and felt at the scene. Seasoned and professional photographers know to look all the way around the view finder first, to investigate all four corners to see if anything that will appear in the photograph might distract from what is being witnessed and experienced. By examining the entire scene, they choose their subject and zoom in.

That's what we do with our prompts and with the kids. The narrower the prompt, the wider the writing. We allow them to zoom in and dig in and talk about who raised them, what they have lost, a sacred place. And we zoom in with them, sitting at small tables helping them replay their tapes so they can write it down.

I believe that teacher and learner are synonymous, but I will admit, my lessons have slowed down. I don't want to say I have seen it all, but I have seen a lot. But this summer, I learned something new from a young man I will call Gregory. Gregory sees and lives in the world differently. He has Autism. Those who don't understand Autism might say that he can't write, because he can't stay focused on the topic and all he wants to do is stay inside his head and draw. But, I discovered that Gregory has the brilliant mind of a fiction writer. Like

92

most fiction writers, he integrates parts of his own life and experience with his third person characters, flawlessly integrating setting, tone, and vivid imagery.

He is a Skylander preparing for battle, a foxboy in the woods who is rescued and then becomes a boy, a super hero with rockets for shoes who soars high above unafraid and looks down and describes to the audience what he sees, a Ninja fighting a mudslinger named Dirt Man.

Gregory didn't want to write at first. He struggled with the narrative tone of the prompts and the 75-minute timeline. But, he did draw and if you asked him what his drawings were, they were clearly addressing the prompt. So as he talked, I wrote. His stories emerged as he drew. Sometimes he would jerk to a halt, look up from his markers, and then look at me and say, "wait, wait, no... this is what happens" and then return just as quickly to his drawing, but changing the words midstream knowing there was a better way to approach the scene.

I have taught students with disabilities in my junior high and university English classrooms and have a ten-year old son with Cerebral Palsy and Autistic tendencies. As a result, I have spent a better part of my education career advocating for students with disabilities. But, I never fully understood the power of "leveling the playing field" and the critical component of success that is possible when a student works one on one with someone.

A key part of our mission with the Memoir Project at the Indiana Writers Center is to give voice to those writers who have a story to tell. But this young man with Autism is the one who gave. He gave all of us who read this book a collection of imaginative writing. He gave me a poignant reminder: Meet writers where they are and let them tell their stories the way they want to tell them. He gave me a stronger and more resolute voice about the power of inclusion. Thank you, Gregory.

Brianna D.

Age 16, Concord

The Glass Beaker

I would like to be known as a glass beaker
Full for my family
Always there for me
Who made me who I am today
Loved me
Supported me
Half full for my best friends
Always there for me
Could be myself around them
Supported my decisions
Helped me make the right choices
Fun to be around
Almost empty for acquaintances
For people who brought my mood down
For people who didn't understand me
For people who didn't know me
For people who never chose to get to know me

***

The Lobster Claw Plant

I am shaped like a lobster claw
I am red, green, and yellow
More red than anything
I dangle like a wind chime
I look like I could snap someone's arm off
Yeah this is me

Schuyler D.
Age 12, Saint Florian

Like a Deflated Balloon

When I saw my brother for the 1st time he was in one of those infant pens and he was crying his head off. Me and my sister were in the front and we were surrounded by family members. It was really funny because a day later my mom's stomach looked like a deflated balloon.

***

Make Her Laugh

I was raised by...
Hazel eyed, kinda short but still taller than me black straight haired woman
a fancy clothes—she has a shirt that makes her look like a cow—purple-loving friendly woman
I have to make her laugh
"Do your chores you're a mess" which is probably true kind of woman.
She's a hard working person that also has to deal with the baby and me.
She's really good with computers but doesn't know how to work the T.V.

Christian A.

Age 13, La Plaza

Nothing is Nothing
Nothing is Nothing, Nothing isn't there.

***

HAPPY

I am always happy.
I like to do fun stuff.
I hang out with my
friends. They think
I'm cool.

***

My Teachers

My teachers cared about me they loved me. They are the best. They used to say to their kids "if we need something just ask them" that way they are caring to every one of us. Even now they still get mad at us they still love us all. They help by a lot, giving things, helping other, and other things. They care about us. They are very helpful with things that we need in our life. They try to ask us if we are going to college.

Dennise D.

Age 12, La Plaza

My Name Is...

My name is white. It's not a Mexican name. It's not a different name. It's not a new name. It's a name you've heard before. My name is annoying, not always the same. People call me by different names all the time. I don't mind really but it annoys me a little bit that I have so many nicknames. My name is not my own. Other people have my name. It's not new, it's old and worn out. It's becoming less common, I think. I don't hear it that often anymore.

***

Change My Hair

I want to change my hair color because I like being different. I don't want to change to brown or blonde or something simple like that. I want it to be like red, purple, or blue. Not green though. I want it to stand out from everybody else. I don't want to be the same as anyone else and I think that changing my hair color will help me out myself from people. I think hair can help tell about a person. The color, the way it's fixed, how someone plays with their hair. And I want to stand out and have my true nature come out. I look quiet and shy because I never feel like talking to people I don't know. But with my friends, I'm as crazy and weird as a monkey on drugs.

Adja "AJ" A.

Age 7, Saint Florian

Raised me

My mom raised me. Gave me education.
She taught me how to say I've got the power!
My Grandma raised me. She taught me how
to write computer it was fun to learn that word.
My dad raised me. He taught me how to dance
and cook and this morning I made eggs and bacon.
My big brother raised me. He taught me how to
walk and run and say non-sense.
My mom is caramel and she has black moles on her,
hair is crazy and when she was a baby she was bald
and now she is older she is 27 and she has a humongous afro.

***

Chocolate

My favorite thing is chocolate. It was brown it is yummy and I found out that it was a container with Hershey's in it and I bought it when I was two years old when I was chewing on it. It was 20 centimeters tall and one inch long. And tasty. It was brown and it has 6 rows of rectangle chocolate. I went to Hershey, Pennsylvania. I eat twelve a year, one each month.

Corrie Herron

Student Teacher, Saint Florian

I was challenged with the idea of describing my experience in one word. Of course, being a stubborn, hard headed woman who grew up surrounded by even more stubborn boys, I could not walk away from this challenge. However, I could not find one word to describe the entirety of the last few weeks—the tears a child shed for the unfortunate fate of her cousin; the excitement a child expressed over a story about his hero, his father; the amazement a child experienced when realizing she filled a whole page with her words, a feat that she had never accomplished before. How could I possibly explain the intense and wholesome emotions and events I experienced within the last few weeks with a simple word? I couldn't. So instead, with the help of fellow intern, Brett Hiatt, a word was created.

Funspiring: the act of inspiring oneself or others through fun.

These children with their bold, simple statements, wild imaginations, and truthful declarations are truly inspiring creatures. Through their honest eyes and even more honest words I became inspired to be a better writer, a better educator, a better person. I allowed their fun personalities to affect my life for the better. I laughed along with them; my heart wept for them with each tear they cried; I read their words, full of desire to know more, to know every detail possible. I learned being sad and admitting that it is okay and I learned being happy five minutes later is a matter of pure strength. They taught me writing is better when laughing and that no matter how the volume in the room, a child's written voice will always be voluminous. With every up and down, I found myself having fun, enjoying the company around me, and loving their words. Thus the explanation for this summer being funspiring. No matter how difficult the writing or upsetting the topic, these children were true to themselves and their ideas, and they always wrote with fun.

Sterling M., Jr.

Age 11, Saint Florian

I remember Mr. Michael talking too much.

Street Legal

I remember the beach the cold water that hits my feet makes me afraid to go any farther because I had a cut on the side of my right foot. I was terrified of Jaws coming for me. I took another step closer to my mother, and she asked me why was scared to come to her. Because the cut on my foot became a pain, and I was scared for my life if a Great White was waiting for me to be dinner. I yelled as loud as I could screaming, "Mommy, Mommy please come get me." My heart was racing at a speed that's not even street legal in any country. I had a very stupid idea tried to swim back to shore but the cut on my foot made it impossible.

***

Who Raised Me?

I was raised by my dear loving mother, grandmothers, aunts, and they all know how to cook very well. I was raised by my dad who taught me how to appreciate when it died. I wanted the dog to live longer with me. Of all the great memories the best of all when we first got him, we play cops and robbers, I'd sneak into his cage and steal his bone and he will come and chase in the yard running them he will tackle me, bark at me once, take the bone will run. I was raised by tough men that will let no one get in their way.

Henry D.
Age 12, La Plaza

Reading is an Experience

I am a book cause I am a tool to people's coconuts. I'm made out of paper, meant to be protected. People in the future will read books like people who do "old fashion" stuff now. And a lot of people won't read me but some will. It makes me hopeful. A lot of qualities that make you a human you can get by reading a book. For instance: entertainment, knowledge, and feelings. Reading is an experience because it is neat.

***

Mom

My mom has always been busy with a big house, 7 kids, cooking, cleaning, paying, working, etc. We go to the YMCA, library, store and Etc. She is an inspiration to me. And a good example. We play games and go to the movies and eat out at places. We go with my dad every Sunday and do something fun. She knows what's right for us even though we don't like it. She tries to do fun activities like Bingo or board games and maybe, if we are really good, puzzles. It's not fun at all 'cause she buys the 1000 pieces.

Chauncey A.

Age 10, Saint Florian

The Best Meal I've Ever Had

The best meal I've ever had was foofu and airo with chicken and African rice. The airo was sticky but still good, but if you eat it alone it tastes interesting, but the chicken was the best. It tastes spicy; the rice was very good, it was fried spicy rice. The foofu was kinda salty, that's why you have to eat it with the airo. It was kinda spicy pretty much all of the African foods are spicy. I was in heaven. I love African food. You can only get airo from Africa; it's a certain grass that is in Africa. Foofu is just dough; it doesn't really take long to make. It was the best meal I've ever had.

***

My White Shoes

My Nike all white shoes I wore to my first baseball game. I ran a mile in my shoes. I played piano in those shoes I did a lot of things in these shoes. They are comfortable. I've won the Basketball Championship in these shoes. I did the moonwalk in my school play in my all white shoes. I'm even wearing these shoes right now. One reason why I wear it every day is because white matches everything. I've had these shoes for 7 months. I got these shoes, since I grew out of all my shoes. It cost a lot of money, well If you have them for 7 months

Roman D.

Age 9, Saint Florian

Biscuits n' Butter: The Original Combo

One day, I was at my granny's house watching Danny Phantom. I thought granny was cooking oatmeal, but she wasn't. So when she said, "Breakfast time!" I was very excited to eat oatmeal but she had something else in mind. So when I looked at my plate I wondered where the oatmeal was. Sooooooo, I said "Where is the oatmeal?" and she said, "Try this." So when I bit this steamy cracked open kind of bread thingamajig I automatically fell in love with it. It basically hypnotized me. I destroyed it in like three seconds. I even ate the crumbs. Then, my granny exclaimed, "Do you want to try biscuits with butter?" and I said, "Yes please!" and then, I just stuffed them in my mouth, crumbs all over my face, I just licked them off into my mouth. I even ate the biscuits when they were cold.

***

Great Wolf Lodge

I asked my mom and dad if I could get a wand and they said "Yes." I was so happy because you could do lots of things with the magical wand, like open treasure chest and find necklaces, and you can play this game where you have to beat the monsters and you have to conquer the monsters to win, and I won the game. I felt like I was invincible and I could beat anyone doing anything. It had dark powers.

Camryn A.

Age 13, Saint Florian

I Was Raised By...

I was raised by a happy strict throw down in the kitchen determined mother who puts god first family second. The woman who keeps me out of trouble, to the woman who hugs and kisses me goodnight to the woman who keeps clothes on back and shoes on my feet. The woman who's always on my case and always with me through thick and thin.

***

My Grandmother

I lost somebody very important to me. Somebody I miss dearly, my grandmother. I lost this woman to kidney failure. The main reason she's gone is because she was an alcoholic. It all started off I was going to bed and my mother stormed into my bedroom saying, "Get your shoes and socks on." Then I said, "Why?" After that she said, "No time to explain." After I got my shoes on I called my dad, "Where are you?" He said, "I'm at the hospital." I got confused and he said my grandmother is in intensive care. My eyes started. I hung up the phone. My mother and I rushed to Methodist Hospital. When I got there everybody said she was alright. I was thinking, "What a relief." My mother and I got back home and went to bed.

The next morning I went to school. I felt so exhausted. At the end of the day, my dad and uncle said my grandmother was gone. I dropped my book bag and I fell to my knees and I started crying a river. Three to four days later the funeral came. I started praying to God, saying, "Why'd you take her from me?" Then the pastor told me everything is going to be alright, and she will be in a better place. Three years, now I'm thirteen years old, feeling great about myself, and every year we visit her tombstone and I know I will see her again.

Darrielle C.
Age 13, Saint Florian

I Lost

I lost my grandma when I was in 4th grade. She was funny. She survived 4 strokes and two heart attacks. She loved cats and dogs. She was very independent and I loved her.

I lost my iPod and I was very mad. My mom was very mad. But good I had insurance so I got a new one and then after a year I had it and it cracked but it still works.

I lost my best friend over a stupid conversation. I knew her ever since I was a baby.

***

Off the Green Grass

Running out on to the field getting into our spots. The fresh green grass under my feet. The taste of hot take sunflowers seeds in my mouth. The pitcher struck the first batter out. The pitcher pitched the yellow hard ball out of her hand. The batter swung the 22 pound bat the ball rolled in between the short stop's legs into left field. The runner running full speed to second the left fielder threw the ball to second base. The second baseman didn't catch it. It rolled towards me in right field I stepped off the green grass into the brown reddish dirt. I guess I tripped over something and fell and scraped my leg it really hurt bleeding a little. My team mates were dying laughing. My leg ached during the whole entire game. I saw this big skid mark on the ground from when I fell in the soft mushy dirt.

Cherif "Ali" A.

Age 8, Saint Florian

My Favorite Food

My favorite food is chebuyap (che-boo-yapp). The last time I ate chebuyap was in Africa. I like my chebuyap with hot sauce and lemon juice. It is so good. It's indescribable. My dad makes it. It's African. He learned how to make it in Morocco. First he combines beef, chicken and lamb in a big pot. He makes rice in a red sauce. He uses African tomatoes. They are brown, like they're sunburnt. Then he puts them in a pot for about 30 minutes. He lets me help him cook. I mix the tomatoes with my hands. When you're done you take it in your hands and squeeze the oil out of it. We keep the oil for donuts. Before they're done my dad cuts some mango. We have that before the food is ready. We say "Bismelahe rackmane reheme" which means, "May Allah (God) bless this food that we are about to eat." The food smells good while it's cooking and then it's done. On special occasions he puts it in a big African bowl, and you eat with your hands, and also you squeeze the oil out with your hands.

***

I was Raised by

I was raised by my mom she helps me with my homework, she devours my cooking she lifts me up when I am down, she helps when I need help, She helped me adjust to my new homes. I was raised by a loving kind hearted African that loves Ice cream dark black skin a nice sharing woman. I was raised by a nice little cousin that I taught karate that I taught her how to play guitar. She taught me how to cut hair. Her name is Hope.

106

Hope L.
Age 8, Saint Florian

Mom, Daddy, Cousin Ali, Papa, Aunt, Great Uncle Tony, Grama

They all raised me by feeding me milk when I was a baby and taught me how to walk and they say, "Hi!" and that I'm good. They teach me how to sing. Ali tried to teach me how to play guitar but I wasn't good. My mom taught me how to play piano and I'm almost good at it. Ali taught me karate, but I took him down. They taught me my spelling words. My grandpa taught about being a firefighter and being a leader by saying thank you and making the world a better place. And they taught me how to cook.

**

Yum!

My mom makes my favorite food...which is fried chicken. I eat the crunchy crusty outside. Then I eat the meat. I use my fingers and they get greasy and I lick my fingers. I help my mom cook it. We first get it out of the refrigerator. Then we put it in a pan. Then we put it inside of the oven and then we put it on the table. We eat it with hot, hot sauce. We eat it with homemade buttered cornbread, corn or corn on the cob or broccoli and with Sprite. For dessert we have vanilla ice cream and chocolate chip cookies every day. We eat chocolate chip cookies every single day. We sit at the table with my sisters and brothers and my dad. I have to sweep the floor. Then I go to bed. But that chicken and hot sauce is the best part. I can taste the hot sauce right now in my mouth. Yum!

Maiya D.
Age 10, Saint Florian

From Crazy to Rad

I was raised by my parent's from crazy to rad. Also to funny then glad. I was raised by my dad from light to bright. I was raised by my mom from quiet to right. I was raised by my parents to be the best I can be from sad to happy no matter what be the best you can be.

I was raised by my parents from crazy to rad. I was raised by my brother from cool to swag. I was raised by my sister from diva to glad. I was raised by god from heaven to earth.

***

My Little Bad Boys

My Adidas are red and white they have laces on them. They feel like warm blankets inside. My shoes are new at first it had a little mark but I scrubbed it off. The shoes got at my front porch because the people from the company shipped them to my house. Something big about my shoes is me getting to wear them and showing them to my friends. Because they look really cool and some people now or then are wearing Adidas. Some people responded that they like the red. Some people said they like the white stripes. These shoes are special to me because they look cool. They're just my little bad boys; they have pizazz to them.

108

Jeremiah H.

Age 6, Saint Florian

Josiah

I was raised by Josiah
Josiah raised me up outside in the grass
We went inside to eat and sleep
He taught me to play to get a good night's sleep
He woke me up, played basketball. He taught me
(My brother) Josiah
Black eyes. He got black eyes
brown skin, white shoes
Me and my brother was playing Xbox
and we take a shower, Then played Xbox
He taught me basketball, Xbox, baseball,
soccer, football, tennis, and volleyball
I Love him

***

Ball and Net

Basketball-blue, green, orange ball and net. It was kinda tight.
It was soft and hard. It was stinky because of sweat.
We play in the backyard. I felt happy.
I played with my brother, Josiah,
and my sister and me

Josiah H.

Age 12, Saint Florian

The Person I am Today

I was raised by people who crack jokes. I was raised by fried chicken, singers, math skills, devil eggs. I was raised by Christians, drummers, I was raised by smart people, important person. I was raised by people black and brown eyes and hair, raised by people who are trustful and respectful to everyone. I was raised by people with style and swag. I was raised by people who play football and basketball, people who agree what I think, people who like the Heat, people who loves their home-town basketball team. I was raised by people who eat a lot, people who loves fried chicken, raised by people who are crazy. I was raised by people who protect me, people who help me when I'm struggling. I was raised by people who laugh sounds like their crying. I was raised by the saying "Get in this house or you won't see tomorrow," I was raised by Artist. I was raised by a family who loves me and care about my future. I was raised by people who like to have fun and people who like to play games. I was raised by people who argue with their brothers and raised by people who like to dance and fart on people. I was raised by a sister who laughs at everything and thinks that she is all that and a bag of Hot Fries. I was raised by a brother who thinks every girl likes him and thinks he is better than me in everything. I was raised by a person who thinks she has to have herself look too cute everywhere she goes. I was raised by a sister who has an attitude when she doesn't get her hair done. Then she said she is going to be lookin' like the ratchets. I was raised by a big sister with attitude and I was raised by my sister having a new boyfriend every week. I was raised by a wonderful family. These people who raised me help me become the person I am today. These things made me very talented and smart.

Nehemiah A.

Age 10, Saint Florian

Raise Me, Teach Me

My mom and dad constantly raise me. My grandma and grandpa raise me too. They taught me well. My aunt raised me. This camp teaches me. My coach taught me well.

This camp teaches me leadership. Standing even when you want to give up you push through. They encourage you to do things. We have Writers Center it helps in writing helping if you want to write when you grow up and just do it for a hobby then for school and college. You write well. These things require patience. Art with a Heart is the same. Karate teaches you self-defense. One of my favorite counselors is Counselor Niki: it teaches you things you do in life. No violence no drugs or tobacco stay in shape be healthy. Karate isn't about fighting; you want to stop the fight.

***

I was Jumpy all Over

I remember going on the Harry Potter ride at Universal Studios. It had you go in Hogwarts where Harry, Ron, and Hermione were talking. They made it snow too. They had talking pictures. My stomach felt weird on the ride. We saw a spider that spit on us; it felt wet. The spider tried to eat us. I was happy while I was on the ride. I was jumpy all over. Harry was taking us through all these obstacles. Harry was on his broomstick. The wind in the building was blowing through me. Finally the ride was over; the ride was awesome!!

111

Tianna C.

Age 10, Saint Florian

Who Raised Me, I was Raised by...

I was raised by God because He made me and He gave life to me. He has been with me through it all. Ever since I was born, He loves me, He feeds me, He keeps me clear, He cares for me, and He stays with me. He keeps me happy even when I'm sad. When I'm feeling down, He cheers me up. And when I'm happy, He's happy.

When I'm sad, He's sad. When I'm cheering, He is cheering. God is my very first dad. God is my very first mom. God is my best friend. God is my brother. God is the Oreo that falls into the milk, sticks with me and never gets eaten. God is my hero. He is still here right next to me. And in my heart. I'm very thankful for my life.

***

I Remember Losing my Grandma

I remember when I went over my Godmother's house to go eat. I asked, "Where is Uncle B?" She replied, "At the hospital," while she stirred up some spaghetti. So when we were eating he came crying and said, "She's gone."

Before she passed it was her birthday.

112

Jasmine A.

Age 11, Concord

This is me

Jasmine
I am as white as snow,
as thick as blood.
When you inhale me, the
smell brings you in.
I have a hint of vanilla
that you can't really describe,
just as the taste of water
does.
My leaves around me scrunch
up as if they were doing
sit ups. My bottom feels like
paper, while the top is very
delicate.
This is me, Jasmine.

***

Marble

Marble is just what I want.
Construct me strong and beautiful, for that is what I am.
Build me for my awesome artistic skills.
Plant Jasmine around me since that is what represents me.
Put me somewhere noticeable, so I may be seen as people pass by.
This is how I want to be built.

Juan A.
Age 13, Concord

THE LEAF

I am purple and black.
I am a leaf
I am a cool designed leaf
I am a dark colored leaf
I feel soft
I am the Bloodleaf's brother

***

'Cause I am a Star Player

I would want to be made of gold
Cause I am a star player at basketball
Good at everything in basketball
Went to the Hall of Fame, the best player in the NBA History
17 championships, I hold the most points
I would want my stance to be my jumpshot
Have my shoes custom made for me
I would want my statue to have my championship rings
Around my monument and my MVP awards
I want my monument to be in downtown
By Bankers Life Pacers home court so when there's a Pacers game
Everybody would come and see me
And remember me and take pictures
And put my jersey on my monument
I am a legend.

Ashantē C.

Age 12, Saint Florian

I was Raised by...

Some I look good type of women,
soul food making women, discipline women,
picky women, Pepsi drinking women, non-self-controlence women,
I love sports type of men
I was raised by some I like sports type of men, soul food eating type men, ice
cream lover type men, I'm fresh type men. I was raised by family who cared
type.

***

My Grandma

I remember when I lost my grandma, she was sweet, kind and a grandma that
was loved on. And the reason why she was a memory is because we had great
time and important memories. I remember when I lost my great-grandma, she
was sweet, loved, and a great-grandma. I remember when I lost my earrings,
they were cute, they were shining brighter than a diamond even though they
was real diamond earrings, plus they were given to me from my grandpa who is
kind and sweet. I was so sad when I lost earrings, grandma, and great-grandma.
These are the best love things I lost with important memories.

Sydney Ba.

Age 9, Saint Florian

My Beauty Spot

My sacred place is the pink soft cozy chair at Art Nails. My feet ooze through the hot, rumbling, bubbling water. My nails are shining like the stars. I feel like a movie star. I felt like a movie star because I felt like I was on the spot light in my dreams so I thought it was real life. I felt like a movie star because on movies I see movie stars with pretty nails like on Bring It On. The nail artist was rubbing my hands it felt won-der-ful, my nails looks bea-u-tiful. When they scrubbed my toes and feet, I was in a new world. It was the middle of the day so that was the moment because I was tired. When I was sitting in that wonderful cozy chair they were painting my nails the color was turquoise with design. When I sit in that cozy chair it reminds me of my memories. My memories were going out of town, spending time with my family, and Cohen. It was on enormous. The cost of it was $25 I think it was worth it. I went to the nail salon with my mother. It smells like nail polish remover. It smells like the best beauty spot in the world. My goal is to go every week so I can get that comfortable seat again and put my feet through that oozing, hot, rumbling, bubbling water.

***

When I spent the night at the zoo.
I remember when I went to the zoo with my school.
I remember when we went to the park at the zoo.
I remember when one of the workers told us about the animals.
I remember about when we saw backstage.
I remember when we slept by the dolphins.
I remember getting splashed.

Darien B.

Age 13, Saint Florian

I was Raised by my Parents

I was raised by a
-medium height kind of mom
-a long natural hair kind of mom
-not a good cook kind of mom
-a very smart person kind of mom
-a mom who works as a teacher
-a caring and sharing mom
-when I had strep throat she took me to the hospital kind of mom
-a stop fighting with your sister kind of mom
-a loved by many kind of mom
-a hot fries eating kind of mom
-a cat hating kind of mom

I was raised by a
-a tall kind of dad
-a big footed dad kind of dad
-a basketball loving kind of dad
-a basketball playing kind of dad
-a glasses wear kind of dad
-a phone loving kind of dad
-a sneakerhead kind of dad
-a outgoing kind of dad

Keiron B.

Age 11, Saint Florian

Who Raised Me

Who raised me? My mom. She raised me good. She fed me and talked to me, and loved me. She fed me chicken, steak, and ribs which I love. We talked about food, chicken, steak, and ribs, which I love talking about. I love food and that is why I love her. I also love her because she takes me places like to school and to swim practice. She watches movies with me.

***

Black and White Adidas

My first black and white Adidas. I always like to have them or because they are very nice. I like my shoes because I went to Georgia in them. I love my shoes so much because when I wear them people say I look nice in them. There was a time I wore the shoes and I went to a friend's house and we walked around the house and I step in poop and my mom told me to throw them away or she said I could clean them so I did I had to wash my hands 9 times. That is why I love my shoes.

Danielle B.

Age 7, Saint Florian

My Mom and Dad

I was raised By my mom and my dad. My mom work at IPS.
and my dad work at VCF.
My mom and dad cook food for me and they take me places.
My dad is tall and my mom is short
I like my mom's smell and my dad's smell.
I like the way my mom Bark Dance and I like the way my dad dance.
My Mom and dad have Black hair.
My mom and dad have nice clothes.
My mom likes to do my nails all the time.
My mom likes to be here at summer camp with me.
My dad likes to be with his friends and family and my mom does too.
I like to watch Basketball with my dad.
My mom and dad have a Black car and a red car.
I like the red car.
They like to go out eat.
Me and my mom like to get our nails done.

***

I remember
I like myself.

Kennedi A.

Age 10, Saint Florian

Who Raised Me

I was raised by Mom, Dad, and Grandfather. I was raised by the American Flag by the National Anthem, and the Pledge of Allegiance. I was raised by the park and my friends. I was raised by my mom's cooking.

***

Mine Had Shoe Laces

In second grade I had got a pair of purple, turquoise and white grapes. They were a size 1. My little brother was 2 years old at that time, he had the same pair of shoe as I did but his had velcro and mine had shoe laces. I did a lot in those shoes like run, play, and go walking on trails. I did a lot of things in those shoes and went a lot of places. A few months later I grew out of them.

***

Sweet Apple Pie

Getting off the bus was great smelling the sweet smell of apple pie. It was a beautiful smell. I loved it; I wanted to get some right away. I was thinking about the crispy crust on the apple pie. It tasted like baked apple.

Mark Latta
Lead Instructor, La Plaza

Like it or not, when we talk about writing, what we really do is wade neck-deep into a paradox of grandiose complexity. It's a dilemma I face every time I enter a classroom or a meeting room of apprehensive authors. On one hand, I believe—I know—they have memories and experiences, desires and embarrassments. They are, simply, human, and because of this I know they have stories to tell, that each head holds lessons of staggering beauty and is capable of the courage that comes from speaking plainly. But if I talk about writing, if I say right up front, "hey you should write that down," I might as well have said, "hey you should take that thought that's near and dear to you and punish yourself for thinking it by engaging in an activity that you believe to be of mind-numbing dullness and punitive retribution." So I believe everyone is a writer because everyone has a story to tell, but I also believe that very few of us want to believe this about ourselves. Paradox.

So when we talk about writing at La Plaza, we don't talk about writing. Instead, we talk about how we may like to write or we may not like to write and that's okay. We talk about how writing can be boring, or trivial, or foisted upon us like a chore akin to cleaning our rooms or taking out the trash, or that it may be something we do in our alone time because it helps us sort things out, and that's okay too. Then we talk about the weekend, what we did, what we didn't do, what we saw, and perhaps who we fervently hoped we would see but didn't. We talk about pain and loss, a grandmother who is no longer with us, a father who can't seem to find his way, a rumor that recently ripped a hole clean through us. We talk about hope and love, a crush that makes our heart skip, our desires to marry or never get divorced, so and so's recent or upcoming quinceañera, our need to play soccer because it's not just a sport it's a way of life and *oh my God could that be used as a metaphor?* We talk about Xbox versus Playstation, about Edward Snowden and the crimes of the United States government, about how a good life is right around the corner, how there are secrets that we need to unload, accomplishments that we wish others recognized, about how everything is ghetto except when everything is beautiful and *oh hey is that imagery?*, and how we love swinging because it makes us feel buoyant like a bird and *wait, is that a simile?* Sometimes we talk about words. Not because there's a vocab test, but because sometimes they jostle around in our mouths and are fun to let go (*cattywampus!*) or they blanket us in comfort (*languid*). Other times, we talk about nothing. Not in the sense of an absence of conversation but rather in the philosophical conundrum of how can there be no thing if we use the word *thing* to describe it.

So when we talk about writing, I try to talk very little about writing. Instead, we talk about life and living and death and gaining and hoping and losing—about being human—and then sometimes, someplace between occasionally and more-often-than-not, I'll say, "that's an amazing story," or, "I really like what you are saying... maybe you should write it down so it sticks around." And when hands start going up and questions start pouring out about how to spell this, the suggested theme, about if we can read this or that, or if it's okay to make a list or a poem or write about something else altogether... When we start talking about that then that's when I know we're talking about writing.

Maybe someday this approach will fail, the bottom will fall out, and I'll have a room full of very disappointed people staring me down and magnifying an extended and awkward silence. But for this year's La Plaza's writing group we talked about a lot and we covered a lot of ground. And wouldn't you know that we wrote a lot too? Like always, the writers at La Plaza teach me a lot each summer and my understanding of the world is better because of them. Sometimes, when we talk about writing we don't talk at all because we're too busy writing it down.

Jalen Se.

Age 12, Concord

When I Die

When I die they are going
To make a monument made of
Black diamonds
So I stood out from the people.
The woman says,
"Oh, look I remember him.
He was the guy good in sports."

And there I am
With the Larry O'Brien trophy
Vince Lombardi trophy
The Stanley Cup
Sprint Cup
And the MVP award
And the Bill Russell MVP award
6 blocks a game
Broke the NBA record in points with 102
I was in 8 Olympics.

Janai S.

Age 8, Saint Florian

Pancake Day

Four to five years ago it was 6:00-7:00 am. It was picture day at my school, Christ Temple Christian Academy, and I was wearing a blue jean jacket, flower shirt, blue jeans, and my wedged black boots. I met up with O'Kayla in our school driveway between 7:45-7:46! It was beginning to be spring. I also saw a man shoveling snow, heard children laughing, and tasted syrup on pancake day because someone flicked syrup on my mouth. It was gross and good. When a photographer took my picture I was excited. Then I had 3 servings of pancakes, 2 each serving. They had mountains of syrup.

The day turned sour but sweet because we had a party. The END

***

My Sacred Place

My sacred place is my couch and I pretend that there's a fire in the fireplace in front of me while I hear the pitter patters of rain in the window pane, while I read my favorite mystery book Pirate School.

My favorite part is my blue snowman covered blanket. I feel like a stuffed caterpillar and lazy. I smelly my mommy cookies while eat them.

I'm in my living room.

I feel sleepy after a while and fall asleep with my special blanket.

The End.

Azhure S.

Age 13, Concord

Braided

I am a Baby tree.
As a kid someone
Braided my Branches
and I liked it so I kept
it that way. So now I can
Show off that kid's work.

***

Golf

I get to golf.
I am on a golf course.
Smells like duck poo
and the smell of freshly cut grass
Fill the air
and the sound of "Fore!" all around.
I have to be on my P's and Q's.
The touch of my glove makes me feel good.
My Auntie is around
and next thing I know is I have a hole-in-one
and then I realize that I am doing my touch down dance.
This will last a life time.

***

My Statue

I would like to be known for my nice attitude and my love for kids.
I would like to be made out of clear plastic and rocks
and I want a time line telling who I am
and what I did
and how I became famous.

Chase S.

Age 6, Saint Florian

Shoes

My favorite pair of shoes is a pair of Nike high tops. The toe of the shoe is gray. It has black mountain stripes. It has a Nike swoosh that is black inside and red on the outside. There are small, red stripes underneath the Nike swoosh. It has a red Nike on the back. It has black shoelaces.

My shoes feel comfortable and soft. They don't rub or hurt me. They stay on my feet all day until I go to bed. Sometimes I wear my low socks or my high socks with my shoes.

On my court, I can dunk in my shoes. We have a medium size goal. Sometimes I play outside and sometimes I play in the garage. I like the way the shoes bend when I play. I like to play with my brother and sometimes friends come over. We play Knock Out.

My dream shoes help me shoot real far away and make it. They take me to California. I want to get the same shoes for my mom, dad, auntie, brother, dad again. These shoes can multiply. Plug in to wall to charge them.

***

Mom and Auntie

I was raised by mom my mom is 22, kinda short and kinda medium.

My auntie helped raise me by letting me and my mom and my brother live with her. She put four hundred dollars in the bank so I could get clothes. She always gave me candy from her work.

She raised me because she taught me to stay on the right side of the street when I ride my bike.

David T., Jr.

Age 8, Saint Florian

Brett

I remember when I first met Brett.
I remember he had on glasses.
I remember he helped me.
I remember he had on a wristband.
I remember he had on fun earrings.
I remember he had on cool Jeans.
I remember he had on a red shirt.
I remember he had on cool shoes.
I remember he had a lot of hair.

***

Lucky Nikes

I remember when I was riding my bike and then I went in my friend's driveway and we played basketball and I was playing my brother and my cousin. Then I went for a three: swish!! You heard it. Then I said so quickly, "It is my shoes." They are Nikes. They are white and also black. They have black, white and stripes. I zoomed down the sidewalk and opened my door! My mom yelled and said, "What happened?"

I said, My shoes, Ma, they are powerful."

Then I went back outside and zoomed to the basketball court and said, "Come on, Lucky Nikes." Then it was my ball I crossed my cousin over. Then I won so that was the best day with my awesome shoes.

127

Michael Baumann

Student Teacher, Saint Florian & La Plaza

Now, I know some men and women who have prose and poetry deep down in their bones and in their hearts; some of them are big, some of them are small, and all of them have stories to voice onto the page. They write what they remember, where they are from, who raised them, and who they want to be. Listen to what they have to say.

I think language, like everything else that is achingly and unapologetically human, is equal parts dangerous and powerful and messy and that everyone has the aptitude and the license to use it. But not everyone knows it, and I feel like my task has been, is, and always will be to help with that.

Everyone needs to know that what you have to say is important.

What all of us have to say is important. Writing can create and empower and heal. In fact, one poet from last summer wrote: "Poems help kids with their problems like a therapist."

This medley of poems and prose from three, major developmental stages—elementary, middle, and high school—represents an emerging generation of artists born almost exclusively after the turn of this century. These artists remind us that creative writing is not merely aesthetic, rhetorical, and evocative—but also powerfully uniting, invitational, and therapeutic.

In the wise-beyond-years words of one of my six-year-old students this summer: "I like writing. It helps me to describe my story. Everyone has a story."

I hope this book heartens you to dip deep down into the prose and poetry of your bones—and to tell your own.

Kelly S.
Age 11, Saint Florian

D. Rose 3.5

My D. Rose 3.5 are Infrared, Black, gray, and neon yellow. Also the shoe strings are infrared too. They look big and clunky because I wear size 11.5, but they are really light. My shoes are not worn out; they are new. Also NBA star Jeff Teague signed them because I was at the Healthplex and he was too, so I asked him for his autograph and he said, "Sure."

Something big was that when I got them I had a game right after and we won. It was exciting because the energy I had from getting the shoes went into the game I played. I almost made half-court shot.

***

Me and My Mom

I was raised by my mom and auntie. Me and my mom had our ups and downs, also she always puts her body in danger for me. Me and my mom have a good relationship. She said she will take a bullet for me.

***

When I Touched an Alligator

When I touched an alligator, I was with my mom, cousin, other cousin and brother. It was fun. I thought it was going to be slimy but it was really dry. Also its claws hurt. He tried to get out of the keeper's hands. He held him tightly; also, he hit the keeper with its tail, I asked the keeper, "Did it hurt?"
He said no, but he is very strong.

Malia Allen

Student Teacher, Saint Florian & La Plaza

Dear Authors,

I say authors because that is what you are. You become authors when you share your stories. When you are stuck, drawing doodles with your pencils, searching your brain to find the right word don't be discouraged. I sit alongside you, watching you dig deep in your hearts and am amazed at the stories you have to share. There are very few things in life that belong only to you, but your story is one of them. Your story is your identity and the world needs it. There are 7 billion people in the world and you are the only one who can share your story with the rest of us.

So when is a good time to write? Write right now! Your story today is different from yesterday and it will change again tomorrow. In our stories we find our identities. We learn, we grow, we change. When we share our stories, we share our lives, and life is meant to be shared.

Write about anything, write about everything, write from your gut. In our gut we find our tears, our laughter, what we have lost, and what we have gained. Your thoughts, ideas and experiences are worth sharing. So go ahead, write about your video games, the crush you can't stop thinking about, and the friend who you lost. Write about your beliefs, good food and good shoes. Write anything, just don't stop writing.

Sharing your life takes courage. It requires you to be uncomfortable and take a risk. When you write you find yourself in places that are scary and long forgotten, but those we can't afford to lose. The stories you carry with you are powerful. We need your stories. We need them to learn. We need them to grow. Your stories are you. The world needs you.

Thanks for sharing your stories with me.

Ahlena S.
Age 8, Saint Florian

My Mom

My mom raised me
she's tall and her
hair is short and black.

She has big eyes.

She cooks me hotdogs
mustard and ketchup
and potato chips.
I get a sprite
soda too. I feel
happy when I eat
this.

When I'm in trouble,
she says sit and time
out.

And she's proud
of me, she tells me.
We watch Spongebob
on TV together and
we laugh!

Nakil S.

Age 10, Saint Florian

When I Was a Fox

I was raised by a fox
when he raised me,
he turned me into
a powerful fox, a tough fox.

I was raised by my mom.
She came out to the woods
and she said to me. "Don't be
running after people
and eating people!"

I met her when I was a fox
and she said, "What
are you doing, foxboy?"
I said, "I'm not your fox."
And that's when she
said to me, "Are you lost?"

And then she found
me and put me
in the chair.
and I had a bib
on. And then
we went to bed.

Jalen St.
I Want to be Made out of Silver

I want to be made out of silver because I love to play basketball
and I want to be posted up with a jump shot
and the reason why I want to be silver
is so someone can see me from a distance
so they want to come over and see my statue
with all the colors.

I'm going to have a paragraph on the front
with my name on the front
also I want to be known
like in history when people notice you
because of books and T.V. and my statue.
I will be known also because I want to go to the (NBA)
National Basketball Association.
I wish I can make it to the NBA.
That is my dream--to make it to the NBA
If I don't, I will do art.

And I will try to get famous on that also.

Kameelah S.

Age 13, Saint Florian

Who Made Me

"You think I'm playin', don't set an attitude" type women. By big Sunday dinner cooking, huge Thanksgiving cooking, joking around type family. I was raised by family, my family, family that had me playin' sports at 4.

I was raised by uncles, uncles that made me tough, that made me good at every sport.

But mainly by a wonderful woman who didn't let me grow up to be bad. Woman who had me try new things although I'm still picky. But I'm still learning. Who made me half of who I am. Who raised me to be a fashion freak.

This fashion freak Virgo has her moments. Her "clean this clean that" moments. Her "let's go somewhere" (fun) moments. A lot of my family calls her big ballin' because I swear she has tons of money… the only person I know who goes to the mall and buys 5 or 6 Coach purses in cash. Who has more than enough Bath and Body Works stuff. Always smellin' good. Who has something ordered to the house every day.

Someone who always has braids in all the time, who jokes a lot but can get feisty at times loves all no matter what, who has a huge heart and does for everyone. Who does not only think about herself, but sometime can be bipolar.

This lovely lady, sometimes over protective, "better not be talkin to no boys" lady is my grandma.

Amari S.

Age 12, Saint Florian

My Grandma

I remember when I lost my grandma. She is important to me because she was the only one besides my sisters who I could talk to about problems with my parents. She was the best cooker in the world. My grandma and I always watched Coming to America. Her favorite movie.

Sometimes if I would mess with my sister she would hit me with a back scratcher. I was sad but I knew it was because she cared.

I felt sad when she was gone and I had no one to talk to.

***

The Day of May 23, 2010

As I walked in the hospital after a long day of school I asked my mom if we could go in the gift shop and get my sister something. We walked in and I found the perfect thing: a teddy that said "welcome to the world, baby boy and mother." I loved it. I bought it and we went upstairs to her room. As we walked in she was half asleep. I went over to where my nephew was. He was so adorable, I wanted to hold him. So I put hand sanitizer on and picked him up. He was as light as a feather. My dad, uncle, and aunt walked in, and saw the precious creature in my hand and almost fell into tears. As we were leaving I started to cry because I was so happy on the Day of May 24, the second day of my nephew's life.
THE END.

Trinity S.

Age 11, Saint Florian

Pushed Off

I remember when my cousin pushed me off the bed, Zion started laughing and my aunt started yelling at him. Then it was my time to laugh, but it happened so fast so I couldn't catch myself. We was just playing. I was holding on to the cover and he said I couldn't sleep in here with his mom so he pushed me off the bed. When it happened so fast I didn't scream because I didn't know what was going on. So he left the room and before he left, he got the pillow and hit me in my face. And I was doing something, my finger went up my nose because I was doing something by my face. Zion was funny he left and I couldn't find him for the rest of the night. Then the next morning he was in the living room, and I said, "where were you last night?" He said "in here." Then I said "no, you weren't, I checked ever where and couldn't find you." So then I started thinking and I thought he was outside talking to one of his friends. But one thing again: he would not do that because the dogs and everything come out at night like the white moon. You know they say if the moon is full then bad things happen.
So then I think he went in his mom's room when I came out because when I stay over at their house, I stay up late. And the dogs broke a lot so that doesn't help. The End.

***

I was Raised by the World

I was raised by the world.
The world that gave me passion and my friends that help me keep going. And basketball that made me find my dream and my mom that loves me and cares. My brother and sister that lead the right path to the right place.

Nuri R.

Age 15, La Plaza

Still and Stoic

He stared blankly at nothing, and his face remained so stoic. Smooth as glass with not even the slightest sign of emotion. Still as a granite statue, he drifted in his own world, in his own head, and with only himself to accompany him. It freaked me out at first. I barely even noticed him 'til I got up to sharpen my pencil. It was like he was frozen in time and his eye were so empty because his mind was somewhere else. He was still and motionless, until the simple word "soccer" was mentioned. And when it did, an explosion happened. His face, once dull, became bright and animated. A smile bloomed across his face as he routed and defended his favorite team and demonstrated special moves with his imaginary soccer ball. And when it was time for us to go outside and play, he'd rip off his pants, revealing his basketball shorts and raced up and down the field keeping close to the rolling ball. And when he finally scored, he'd fling his hands in the air whooping and hollering his victory to his friends.

***

Not a Blockade

My past doesn't define me. No way in the world would I let that happen. No, no, I won't let that be a barrier to my future. Not a blockade, or fortress, or even a measly picket fence. I define my future. My choices define me. My goals & my hopes define me. The love for my passions defines me, but not my past. No. No. Not my past.

Everett S., III

Age 12, Saint Florian

Kind of Aunt I Love

I was raised by a
cook master
Finger lickin' chicken,
juicy meat and crunchy crust
in my mouth kind of aunt.

An apron/dress wearing kind
of aunt.

#1 fan of basketball, loud
Screamin', joyful cheering
kind of aunt.

And that's the kind of aunt
I love.

***

Basketball

On a Saturday morning I went to Eastern Star church. As I walked into the church I felt a cold breeze down my back. As I walked in the gym I looked up. . . Then down. The fan was spinning slowly as I walked in.

My basketball dropped as I put on my sneakers. My blue and gold Hyper Fuses. As I took them out of my bad I unraveled the laces and pulled out the tongue. As I laced them up I remembered a saying from Michael Jordan like

"I can accept losing, and that's ok!"

Bryan M.
Age 8, Saint Florian

The Birthday Shoes

I remember when I first got my shoes. On my birthday. I got a box before I went to school. I wondered what was in it. I opened the box; there were shoes. There was a sign that said Converse on it. They had stars on every side and on the back. It had Converse on the back. They had black shoe strings and the shoes were Black too. When I put them on, I felt cool. When I got to school, everyone said that they were cool. My mom said I only get to pick one friend. Kaleb or David. I picked Kaleb. We went to Chuck-E-Cheese. We came Back to the house. We ate cake and opened presents. I got a new DSI game. Me and Kaleb played it all night. We had fun!!!!!

***

Hot, Hot, Hot Wings

I like hot wings. When I tasted it, my mouth was really hot. My dad made them. I like them really really really really really really really really really hot. They were hot, but I ate 3. I didn't need water. The sauce covered my mouth. And I had to clean myself up. The French fries were salty. They were fat and greasy. They were hot. The brownie was chocolaty and warm. It was chewy and sticky. The ice cream cooled it down.

Writing Prompts

Below find the writing prompts for each of the three sites served by Building a Rainbow in 2013. We share these prompts in the hope that you too will write and have your voice be heard.

***

I Remember

Write "I remember..." and the first memory that comes to mind. Keep doing this for 3-5 minutes, repeating "I remember" each time, writing no more than two—three, tops—sentences per memory. Write quickly, don't worry about spelling, punctuation, or the order in which the memories come. (They will be all over the place!) Don't worry about the memories being silly or inconsequential, either. Just remember. Because the flow of memories comes from your right brain, most if not all of the memories will have a visual, even cinematic quality. (Note: Writing "I Remember" every time keeps the writer in the visual part of the brain when students can write fast enough to get a rhythm going. Listing shifts the task to the left brain, which will try to bring order to it too soon.)

Count the number of memories you have. Consider each one the first draft of a piece of writing you might develop. Then choose one that you want to write about.

Note: Discourage students from writing about memories that cover a long period of time. For example, instead of writing about a vacation to Florida, choose a moment from that trip.

Choose one of the memories to work with.

Repeat the "I Remember" exercise for the memory, writing down as many details about it as you can remember.

Freewrite the story of that memory, using the details you remembered (it's okay not to use all of them) and feeling free to add new ones that come into your mind. If you get stuck, look at your list of details and just start writing about any one of them. Don't worry about spelling, punctuation, organization—any of that.

Note: "Tricks" to help students overcome anxiety include writing in the present tense, writing the memory as if they're writing it in a letter to someone they love, or writing down the story of the movie in their mind.

Read your draft. Underline sentences and phrases you like, cross out things that you don't need. Add details that will make the story stronger and clearer. Does something in the middle seem like a good beginning? Move it up. In fact, you might even cut the drafts into chunks and fool around, rearranging them. (Note: If there's time, students can exchange papers and ask questions and make observations to help each other set revision tasks.)

Standing in the Image
(Adapted from an exercise by Lynda Barry)

Close your eyes, relax, breathe deeply, and let your memory come into your mind. In your mind's eye, look straight ahead. What do you see? Look to the left, to the right. Look down, up, behind you. What do you hear in the scene? What do you smell, taste, touch?

Quickly make a list of all of the details you noticed. Then freewrite about the picture in your mind. You don't have to use all of the details you wrote down and you can feel free to use new details that you remember as you write.

Note: this exercise can be used alone to generate freewriting and/or used in the "I Remember" exercise before starting the second set of "I Remembers" about the chosen memory or after the freewriting as a way to generate new details for the second draft.

I Remember, I Am, I Dream, Deep Down I Know...

Write, "I am... " and finish the sentence. Keep going for 2-3 minutes, repeating "I am" each time. Write, "I dream..." and finish the sentence. Keep going for 2-3 minutes, repeating "I dream" each time. Write "Deep down I know..." and finish the sentence. Keep going for 2-3 minutes, repeating "I dream" each time. Order each set the way you want them to be into a poem. It's okay to leave some out and add some new ones.

What Have You Lost?

Make a list of things you've lost. They might be toys or clothes; people or places. An important competition you lost. Anything. They might be things you loved and felt sad about losing or things you didn't like and were glad to get rid of—though maybe you got in trouble for losing them. Pick one of those things to write about. You might write about how you got it, how you lost it, how you used it (if it's an object) and/or a memory (if it's a person.

Shoes

Think about all the shoes you ever had and pick one pair that you really, really loved—maybe still love. Close your eyes and see the shoes in your imagination. What to they look like? What do they look like? What color are they? Do they have laces, buckles, snaps, Velcro? How do they feel, smell? Do they make a sound? Now write about something you did, someplace you went, or something that happened when you were wearing your shoes.

Who Raised You?

Read aloud the poem by Kelly Norman Ellis "Raised by Women." Think about all the people in your life who have helped to raise you. They might be family members, neighbors, teachers, counselors, friends. You can also choose to think about just one person who raised you. Think about the kind of details Ellis uses in her poem, then make a list of details about the person or people who raised you. Be specific. Use creative language, like Ellis did. Use the details to write a poem that begins with "I was raised by..." You don't have to use all of the details. Feel free to add new details that you think of while you're writing.

Sacred Places

Read "The Sacred" by Stephen Dunn. Think of a place that is sacred—or special to you. Write down some things about the place. Are there smells, sounds? What are the colors there? What happens in the place? Are you there with people, or alone? "Do the Standing in the Image" exercise to help you see it in your mind's eye. Then describe the place and/or write about something that happened in the place.

Toys

Close your eyes and imagine rows of shelves with all the toys you ever played with in your whole life on them. Since we're imagining, the toys can be any size—large or small—and they're lined up very neatly. Choose one toy and take it off the shelf. Keeping your eyes closed, look at it closely. Feel it, smell it? Does it make any kind of noise? Write about playing with that toy. How does your playtime begin? Where do you play with it? Is there anyone playing with you? Then write the story of playing with the toy.

Good Food

Read aloud Sandra Cisneros's poem "Good Hot Dogs." Think about a time you had something really good to eat. Close your eyes and see the food in your mind's eye: What did it look like? How did it smell? How did it feel inside your mouth, on your tongue? Was it easy or hard to eat? Did you pick it up or eat it with a fork or spoon? Was it cold? Hot? Spicy? What kind of spice? Was it sticky? What did you say about the food? Where were you when you ate the food? Were there people with you? Tell the story of eating the food in a poem. You don't have to use all of the details you wrote down and you can feel free to use new ones you remember as you're working on the poem.

Many young writers have a favorite food often related to a family recipe, but they aren't aware of how the food is made or prepared. As a variation for the food prompt, ask students to "interview" their family to discover how their favorite foods are made. Ask them to compile recipes—recipes are often very poetic and narrative when viewed in a new light. Often, these foods give way to stories of family history and triumphs. What do these recipes and food stories say about a student's culture and family history?

My Name

Read "My Name" from *The House On Mango Street*, by Sandra Cisneros. Now, think about your name. Do you know what it means? If so, does it describe who you are? If not, what does your name mean to you? Does your name make you think of a color? A person? A Place? What do other people think about your name? Is there a story about your name? Why did your parents give you that name? Has anything funny ever happened because of your name? If you could change your name, what would your new name be? Why? How does that name describe you better? Write a poem or in which every line begins with "My name..." Each time you write it, say something else about your name. The things you write can be real or imaginary.

Lists

In the words of Umberto Eco, "we like lists because we don't want to die." While this sentiment is likely too heavy for young writers, it gives way a powerful truth about lists: while we often use them as useful brainstorming exercises, lists can also be very revealing final drafts. Writing lists also comes natural to most writers. Perhaps the most interesting aspect about lists is not what they contain, but what they don't contain and what this reveals about the list creator. For example, making a playlist for a special someone reveals not only how the author feels about the intended recipient, but also demonstrates an ability to cross over into a very controlled multi-modal composition.

List of Suggested Lists as Writing Prompts:

"Things I Want to Do in Five Years"
"Things I Never Want to Do or Have Happen to Me"
"Things I Wish Someone Knew About Me"
"Top Ten Songs to Play During A Perfect Day"
"The Top One Thing I Believe"
"Top Things I Never Want to Write About"

Found Poem

This is a writing exercise that usually doesn't feel like writing and that's probably why it is so successful. Gather a handful of magazines and newspapers (any published writing will do), or better yet—ask students to bring in old magazines, mailings or newspapers of their own. Using a sheet of construction paper, scissors, and glue (or tape), ask students to comb through the pile of texts to assemble a story.

Sometimes it's helpful to suggest a theme or provide an example of your own, but many times it's not. While many students may find this vague instruction to be initially confusing because they aren't used to writing by assembling pictures and pre-printed text together, most eventually begin to find patterns within the assembled texts and gravitate towards these patterns to fashion a story together. In the years we've used this prompt, we've never had a student who didn't "get it" or eventually loose themselves in the joy of assembling a narrative.

Poem About a Favorite Summer Activity

Write a poem describing one of your favorite summer activities. Your favorite pastime might be anything you enjoy: traveling, playing a certain sport, hiking in a park, visiting relatives or eating a particular food. You can write about how this activity is the same each time you do it, or you can describe a particular memory you have of this activity. Use strong action words.

Poem About Nature

Write a poem describing your walk through the Marian University Ecolab or focusing on one particular plant or animal that you find interesting on your walk. Use details that paint a picture and appeal to the senses. Try to also include at least one imaginative comparison.

A Persona Poem

As you walk through the Garfield Conservatory, choose a plant or animal that you find interesting and that you identify with in some way. Think about how both of you are alike. Then write a poem in which you speak for it. You might describe what you look like, what you like to think about or do, what irritates you about people, what you dream about at night, what makes you afraid or happy, or anything else that you want to say for this plant or animal.

A Self-Portrait Poem

Write a poem that tells the reader how you would like to be drawn (or painted) or how you would like to be portrayed in a sculpture or monument. What materials should your monument or painting be made with? What colors? What details should be included? Your poem should reveal who you are: for example, what you like or don't like about yourself, what you want people to know about you and remember, what you think is important in life or what you feel like inside.

Will Watson

My work is a celebration of self, combined with the collective world around me. Growing up in an urban environment, my experiences offered me an understanding of struggle. Hip Hop culture and people I encounter help me understand what hope looks like, dreams of success, and how to make the best of any situation. Images I illustrate reflect this environment, causing it to be very fun and playful at times. The content and visual approach of my work is inspired by strong meaningful emotions that portray a positive image of my heritage, history, and culture. Imagery in my work is connected to my own personal growth and success story as it relates to the African American experience.

While creating work, I focus on basic aesthetics of art such as color, form, space, and motion. Frequently I paint straight out of the tube, allowing the paint to mix an array of colors directly on the canvas. Colors I use in my work often reflect the influences of graffiti, surrealism, and abstract expressionist art. The overall structure of my work moves with rhythmic shapes and patterns, influenced by my careful mark making and assemblage. My compositions emphasize values and texture. Shapes and patterns I use originate from an inspiration of music and spoken word poetry. The personal connection I have with music and poetry expresses an emotional attachment to my work. A majority of my work is influenced by my own personal life, feelings, and thoughts. Occasionally I create work that is purely a documentation of my emotions, leaving the viewer to come up with their own perception. While other times I find influence from life and all of its imperfections.

When looking at my art, I would like to invite my viewers to step into my world; I want them to feel the emotions depicted in the images. My sole purpose as an artist is to make work that is self-satisfying. Self-fulfillment is the greatest joy for me as an artist. I want my viewers to laugh, sing, dance, protest, celebrate, empathize, groove and vibe to the rhythms expressed in my work. I truly feel if the outcome of my work is pleasing to me there will always be somebody else who will enjoy my work as well.

Acknowledgements

The Indiana Writers Center gratefully acknowledges the support of these organizations and individuals:

Faith Cohen
Jennifer Jensen
Mark Latta
Michelle Maslowski
Emily Montague
Vanessa Russell
Kate Shoup
Julianna Thibodeaux
Joan Warrick
Hud and Diane Pfeiffer

Rebecca Huehls
Darolyn Jones
Claire Lee
Laurane Mendelsohn
Steven Pettinga and Mike Byrum
Jennifer Shoup
Steve Shoup
Vicki Townsend
Samiha Zammouri

Saint Florian Center
The Indianapolis Foundation
Marian University
Indiana Arts Commission
Summer Youth Program Fund

Lilly Endowment
Hoover Family Fund
Concord Neighborhood Center
Arts Council of Indianapolis
La Plaza

Index

Ja'Len K	62	Nuri R	137
Kaleb K	71	Anthony R	14
Mar'kayla K	64	Michelle S-R	5
William Lagunas	89	James Sandberg	6
Mark Latta	121	Everett S. III	138
Hope L	107	Leeann Sausser	68
Malaki L	65	Jalen Se	123
Noah M	66	Janai S	124
Christopher M	67	Azhure S	125
William (Will) M	70	Barb Shoup	ii
Noemi M	77	Chase S	126
Anthony M	72	Kelly S	129
Bryan M	139	Ahlena S	131
Bryce M	73	Nakil S	132
Ciaran McQuiston	38	Amari S	135
Elyjah M	74	Trinity S	136
Stephanie M	75	Jalen St	133
Andrew Mo	76	Kameelah S	134
Sterling M. Jr	100	Angeles Noelle S	31
Amani M	86	Jordan T	32
Breanna N	87	David T. Jr	127
Eric P	82	Davia T	9
Joshua P	81	Dayron T. Jr	10
LaNiyah P	80	Julianna Thibodeaux	83
Trinity P	1	Cortez T	11
Imari Q	2	Darrick T	12
Salvador R	3	Eiondra T	15
Desmond R	4	Marquia T	16
Taiche R	13	Anton T	19

Anthony T	20
Lenabel T	21
Natalia V.C	22
Tamara V	25
Shari Wagner	55
Alannah W	28
Kamon W	29
Kayla W	30
Xaveon W	13
Roderick W. II	34
Zack W-D	37
Celeste Williams	47
Morgan W	40

www.ingramcontent.com/pod-product-compliance
Lightning Source LLC
Chambersburg PA
CBHW081550040426
42448CB00016B/3280